LITTLE FRIEND

LITTLE FRIEND

EMILIO ROJAS

illustrations by Valdés Galindo

ELEMENT

Rockport, Massachusetts ● Shaftesbury, Dorset
Brisbane, Queensland

Original Spanish © Emilio Rojas 1984 and 1987
Translation © Element, Inc. 1992
Translated by Delbert Riddle with Anthony Edkins
Illustrations © Valdés Galindo 1992
Photographed by Lorena Alcaraz and Bernardo Arcos

Published in the U.S.A. in 1992 by
Element, Inc.
42 Broadway, Rockport, MA 01966

Published in Great Britain in 1992 by
Element Books Limited
Longmead, Shaftesbury, Dorset

Published in Australia in 1992 by
Element Books Ltd for
Jacaranda Wiley Ltd
33 Park Road, Milton, Brisbane, 4064

Designed by Peter Bridgewater/Annie Moss
Typesetting by Vanessa Good
Printed and bound in Great Britain by
The Bath Press Ltd

Library of Congress Cataloging-in-Publication Data
Rojas, Emilio.
Little Friend.
Translation of Pequeño Hombre and Aprendiz de Pintor.
Includes illustrations by Valdés Galindo.
I. Rojas, Emilio, 1948-   Aprendiz de Pintor.   English.   1992.
II. Title.
PQ 7298.28.0343P4713 1991
91-30120 863—dc20 CIP

British Library Cataloguing in Publication
Data available

ISBN 1 85230 281 X

This book is dedicated to

CRISTINA GALLEGOS

~

TABLE OF CONTENTS

THE GREATEST TREASURE

    TWILIGHT'S last rays revealed Little Friend, gathering fruit for his journey, and an old man, ancient enough to be all humanity's father. From the watchtower of night, the stars secretly observed them as they sat by the campfire, wrapped in their loneliness.

That night Little Friend had undreamed of dreams. When he awoke, he felt the old man's absence. Trying to remember his dreams, he heard the sage saying: "I am the guardian of the greatest treasure anyone has ever possessed. Once every hundred years I appear in order to discover if anyone has the right to the treasure. Today you have been chosen and I will give it to you. Climb the mountain that stands before you and take it!"

Little Friend climbed for three days before he reached the top. He was awestruck by a universe he had never seen before.

Radiant light beamed from a grotto. From the depths of the cave, shining through stalactites, words written with sunlight proclaimed:

> *The heart is the center.*
> *Dispersing into prisms,*
> *It forms a star,*
> *From whose golden light*
> *Life's meaning is born.*
> *This star is Love,*
> *And you are the light*
> *That makes it shine.*

LITTLE FRIEND
AND HIS QUEEN

◆

L ITTLE FRIEND was blessed with a Queen
who appeared with the rising moon. She
was his consolation, his peace and the
source of his rebirth at the death of each day.

His Queen was the very sweetness of fruit, and her
voice was a song to nourish the soul. Her smile was as
exuberant as an ocean wave and sparkled like a
fountain. Her heart was a fertile valley. The colors of
every part of her angelic body were perfect in every
way. She dressed in the robes of the dawn and the
spring. Her eyes were like the endless sky, and they
reflected an infinite horizon. She smelled like every
fragrance of every flower, and her walk was as delicate
and as majestic as wind rippling through a field of
wheat. She was a sight that filled the heart with joy.

But Little Friend complained that he only saw his
Queen when the moon took pity on him and carried
him to the hidden world of dreams. Though dying of
love, Little Friend never found his loved one when he
was awake. For he never looked for her in reality, but
he sought her only in dreams.

THE STREAM

ONCE, on the shores of thought, I watched the movement of a Stream. The Stream stopped and asked me: "Are you learning anything, Brother, from the way I flow by?"

"More than learning something," I answered with an empty smile, "I'm looking at how you suffer. Your suffering must be very great! You start life as a beautiful spring, but your journey takes you to the sea where you die."

The Stream stopped murmuring and replied: "Don't become even smaller than you are, Brother, by thinking others are as empty as you. It's true I flow to the sea. But look around you. See the flowers that grow where I've passed."

THE WANDERING STAR

ONCE I rode on a wandering Star. In days gone by our paths had crossed, and we had decided to travel on together.

In one of those moments when we were both deep in our own thoughts, the Star turned her silvery face toward me and asked: "Little Friend, aren't you afraid, knowing that my fiery tail could reduce you to ashes whenever I wanted?"

I paused and then replied: "If I'm afraid, then I'll never find what I'm looking for. And if you're my sail, and I'm your rudder, aren't you yourself afraid? For I could steer you off course and make you crash and shatter into little pieces."

She answered with silence, a long look and then a friendly smile. We continued to travel together, treasuring in our hearts the dawn's fruits we gathered along the way.

THE PARTY

*I*T was a holiday. Soul rushed to and fro seeing to things and arranging a place for Atmosphere and her orchestra, who had just arrived.

Distant birdsong and a chink of light through the curtains announced the coming of Her Majesty the Moon. There was a knock at the door. Heart, dressed formally, went to open it.

The first guest was Loneliness, followed by Absence and her friend Sadness. Paper and Pen, always great friends, arrived next. When all had taken their places, a great commotion ensued. Ideas, accompanied by Letters and Words, made a grand and tumultuous entrance.

Just then, the orchestra's conductor, Silence, tossed his magnificent head of hair and tapped his baton. The music began. Suddenly Memory appeared with his loving sweetheart Melancholy clinging to his arm.

Checking his guest list, Heart closed the door. "Wait a minute," cried Little Friend.

"My most important guest hasn't arrived yet!"

"Who is that?" asked Heart.

"Love," answered Little Friend.

Heart looked at Little Friend with the tender concern of a protective parent. He shook his head slowly and patiently and then, after a moment, replied: "But Love arrived long ago."

Little Friend, doubting what Heart had told him, dashed off in search of Love.

Heart had not deceived him. Love was there. But he looked more like someone from the underworld than a heavenly guest. He sat huddled on the floor in a corner, his hands between his knees, his head tilted back against the wall. His gaze was empty, and his eyes overflowed with tears, forming a pool of hope.

THE KING

A KING walked in a forest along a river path surrounded by flowers and birds. While he was strolling along, the sun hid itself behind the mountains.

In the deepening darkness, he could not see the path beneath his feet, and he stumbled and fell. While he was trying to get up, he hurt himself.

His cry of angry frustration shattered the silence. "I am King, and I order the darkness to depart!"

The Night echoed in reply: "Do not complain, Little Friend. Without my darkness you would never know the stars, and you would never appreciate the light."

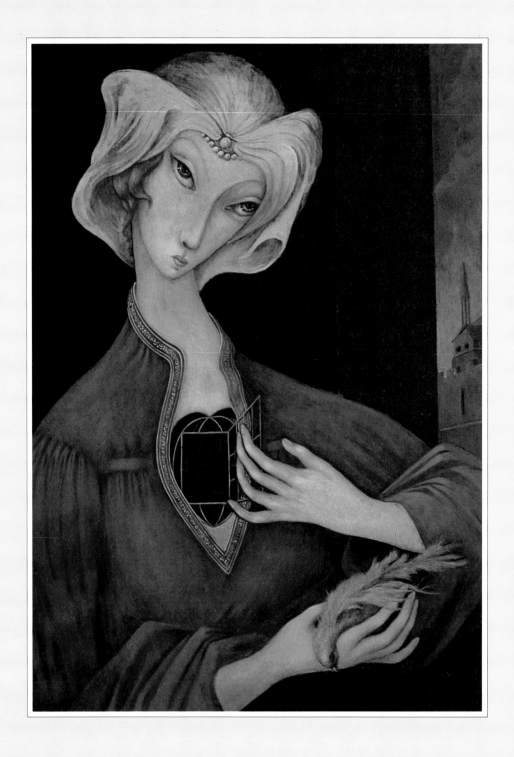

THE BEAUTIFUL FLOWER

ONE day, in the midst of virgin countryside, a radiant Flower was miraculously born. The mountain peaks surrounding her conversed with the passing clouds. The land was a rainbow patchwork quilt woven of wildflowers, grass and shrubs. The wind, rippling through the quilt, was laden with an infinite variety of birdsong.

The more the Flower grew, the more beautiful and fragrant she became. Eventually she grew proud of her gifts.

One evening a Caterpillar began to climb her elegant stem. "Stop!" she exclaimed arrogantly. "How dare you climb something as fragrant and beautiful as I?" Saying nothing, the Caterpillar retraced its steps and crawled beneath a nearby branch. Feeling the pressure of time, it began weaving its sunbeam threads into a sturdy home.

Time passed.

A Bumblebee tried to collect pollen from the beautiful Flower. Seeing it coming, she exclaimed: "Stop! Don't you dare touch me." The Bumblebee hovered in the air for a few seconds, looked at her, turned and flew away, becoming a tiny dot on the horizon.

Time passed.

One day an unusual Butterfly emerged from the Caterpillar's house. Admiring it, the Flower conceitedly announced: "I offer to you my fertile gifts. Take them to the four corners of the world. Cover the earth with my beauty and fragrance."

Wrapped in an aura of peace, the Butterfly replied: "Yesterday you possessed gifts that time has now decayed. Fertile you may be, but I will not be guilty of allowing flowers like you to be born." And off the Butterfly went in search of others not so vain.

Looking at herself and remembering her attitude, the Flower was the very image of defeat. Her defeat was confirmed when, gingerly reaching inside her breast, she discovered that her heart's wings would no longer open wide.

THE SAGE

—— ◆ ——

AN old man sat on top of a hill. His long white beard and peaceful face gave him the appearance of wisdom. He looked down on a village that no longer resembled the village he remembered.

One day, the old man journeyed down from the hill and knocked at the door of a house, hoping to be given a little bread and water. Instead, he was invited inside to share the finest meal the young couple living there could provide.

Over dinner, they asked the old man who he was and what he did. He admitted that he was a native of their village but that for many years he had traveled foreign lands in search of wisdom.

His admiring listeners begged him to share his most profound insight. After a moment of sober reflection, the old man answered: "To be in each moment and to be present in everything you do."

Silence descended, broken only when the young couple said: "Bless you for returning to teach us about wisdom. We used to think wisdom meant Love."

Unable to comprehend such a complicated word, the old man departed in search of further understanding.

THE WEAVER'S APPRENTICE

—— ◆ ——

I REMEMBER that as a child I couldn't wait to own my first pair of long pants. Then it was a coat and tie. Still later a large hat, a warm shirt and a cane.

After a lifetime of rushing through all my days, I finally noticed that time doesn't hurry along. It flows at a pace that allows it to weave beautiful Springtimes.

Now that I know this in the Winter of my life, let me weave beautiful Springtimes.

THE PAINTER'S APPRENTICE

———— ◆ ————

WHILE traveling through life, Little Friend came to know a wanderer called the Painter's Apprentice. This man was always surrounded by people asking him about paintings he had yet to paint.

The paintings he described were so ethereal that they resembled music forming in air. The Painter's Apprentice said that the timeless and the eternal could be captured through feeling and sensitivity, releasing the soul toward the spirit's essence. He described a painting of dancing in which the body was a connection between the earth and the soul.

Then he envisaged a painting made of embossed letters – each one a word, a sentence, a prayer, a book wherein the author had woven tales out of history, imagination and dreams. He wanted to create a painting in which the brush strokes and colors were the essence of all that could be ordered and balanced. He also described a painting in which the motifs were feelings formed from the tiniest elements of life in the depths of the interior world.

Then the Painter's Apprentice said that his true aspiration was to paint people. Not those who claimed greatness and then sank into the mud of oblivion. Not those who spoke hurtful words or performed acts of hypocrisy. Not those who used others to climb to the top or exchanged love's treasures for trinkets, popularity or material wealth.

The people he wished to paint were simple folk without disguise, those who were at once ethereal and steadfast. They were the ones whose wings could carry them to the horizon.

Such people teach us how to walk through the valleys of each day. They draw a smile from our hearts and say to us: "To live is to learn what we were, what we are and what, with the setting of the sun, we shall be. To live is also to understand the human being and the universe, and thus to become a maker of stars. To live is to look at our outstretched hands, one of which contains nothing, the other, everything. To live is to be the immortal energy and light that flow from the Rose of the Heart."

This was how the Painter's Apprentice talked about the pictures he was going to paint. But he never made a single sketch. Curious to see what these paintings would look like, Little Friend followed the Painter's Apprentice for a long time. Finally, when the Painter's Apprentice produced nothing, Little Friend, disappointed, left him. After some time had passed, Little Friend realized that the word was the brush of the Painter's Apprentice and each person part of his canvas.

THE TAX DODGER

◆

*A*s time passed and night after night no lights appeared in the heavens, the worried King summoned his astronomers. But they couldn't explain this strange phenomenon. Days ran into weeks, and the monarch became more and more anxious. He finally consulted a seer of great renown, who told him that the tax collector could provide the answer to this mystery.

The tax collector was summoned at once but denied any responsibility. The King believed him. He considered his tax collector honorable and truthful, if a bit overzealous in dealing with those who had failed to pay their taxes.

But as the tax collector was about to leave the palace, he paused. With an incredulous expression on his face, he scratched his chin and muttered: "Could it be true?"

The voice of the King filled the great hall, and its echo asked: "Is there anything wrong?"

The tax collector turned back. It was slowly coming back to him. "There was something, Your Majesty, during the course of my official duties. One afternoon, I came across a man who claimed his work brought no income, so he couldn't pay taxes. Intrigued, I asked him what he did. He told me he was the Polisher of Stars."

"And what did you do?" asked the King.

"I thought he was making fun of me and of the kingdom and trying to avoid paying taxes. I had him jailed."

The King commanded that the Star Polisher be freed immediately. "He must be paid what he's owed and given personal compensation. In fact, he deserves honors. For this man not only polishes our stars, he also illuminates our dreams."

THE QUEST

"My quest began only recently," Little Friend told the man who had stopped him. "I'll tell you how it all started.

"It so happens I have been blind since birth. But in my blindness I learned to see in the dark. I found ways of inventing colors and seeing smiles on people's faces.

"I should also mention that my hearing never developed. Yet I could hear the sounds of the spoken word, the laughter of little children and the songs of birds flying free.

"The sense of smell was also closed to me, but I recognized each person's scent, the freshness of clean streets, the pure air of the forests and rivers.

"My sense of taste had lain dormant, but in my dreams I savored delicious meals and the best wines. I made the most of these and other pleasures.

"Yes, my heart was locked inside seven strongboxes, but even within such a prison, my desires, wishes and feelings were sublime. Humanity was a single person and the world a garden of colors and fragrances.

"But then one day, along came one of those people who try to heal everybody's pain and, feeling sorry for me, he cured me of my infirmities.

"Since then, I have been searching for him everywhere. I want to beg him for an antidote to the cure he gave me. I cannot bear such good health."

THE PLANT AND THE JOURNEYMAN

*I*N the deepest part of the forest, a Plant of many colors lived. One morning she was surprised to see a man walking along, admiring the surroundings. When he drew near, she stopped him. "Good sir, be kind to me. Take me with you, and I will bring joy and beauty to your home."

After a brief pause for thought, the man replied: "You are lovely and fragrant, and I would like to do what you ask. But I am a journeyman, and I wouldn't be at home to look after you. Besides, you are in your element here. It would be best if you stayed." And with that, he continued on his way.

Just as he was about to disappear into the forest, the Plant cried out to him tearfully: "Please don't leave me here. I will die soon in these harsh conditions." Moved to pity, the man came back and took her home with him.

As time passed, the Plant began to blame herself. "Why did I come here? Confined to this pot, I'm not like my sisters in the woods who can grow to maturity." Even as she was speaking, she was filled with fear. For she saw the man who took care of her pick up his journeyman's bag and leave the house to return to his traveling.

THE MUSIC MAKER
◆
for Alicia Urreta

ONCE asked a brilliant composer how she managed to achieve the richness of her music.

"It's easy," she said. "I simply transform myself into pure feeling in relation to an image or an idea. Then I only need to stretch out a sensitive hand and harvest the notes that are all around me. I feed the notes into my head as if it were a vessel. Then, like an organ grinder, I turn the handle of my heart. With each turn, from my heart comes the music I give to you."

THE ONE-EYED MAN
IN THE LAND OF THE BLIND

A GLIMPSE of the infinite was reflected in the old man's gaze, and the stillness of the stars was mirrored in his face. He was surrounded by an array of people, both young and old, too numerous to count. They had come from the far corners of the earth, hoping someday to become just like him.

The faraway look on the master's face began to change, and little by little his attention returned to those around him. His peace of mind was reflected in his voice as he asked: "Is it true that the one-eyed man in the land of the blind is king?" Almost in unison, many around him replied: "Yes."

Unperturbed, he asked the one most vehement: "On what do you base your opinion?"

"Because his vision is better than that of any of the others. That makes him superior," was the immediate reply.

"The first part of what you say is correct," answered the wise man. "But his eyesight wouldn't make him superior. Could such a king govern a people so unlike himself? I don't think so. He wouldn't understand their strange world. The king and his subjects would be speaking different languages, and the lack of communication would lead to chaos for all.

"In the land of the blind, the one-eyed man would not be a king. He would be an idiot, a complete misfit."

THE TRANSACTION

AT the gates of his mansion, a very handsome, very rich young man waited for a peddler. Seeing him in the distance, he shouted: "Peddler! Peddler! How much does love cost?"

As he approached, the peddler replied: "I don't sell love. I give it in exchange."

"Many have told me that there is nothing better than love. Come in and look at what I own. Take whatever I have."

"I don't exchange love for material things," said the peddler.

"For what then?" asked the young man.

"Only pure tears born of grief," replied the peddler.

"Do I have to pay now?" the young man asked.

"When the right moment arrives," answered the peddler.

"All right, then give me love now," said the young man, inwardly exulting, "What a great bargain! Now that I will have love, added to what I already possess, I will surely know little of grief and tears."

As he slowly moved away, the giver of love murmured to himself: "Poor thing! Your heart is so young. Little do you realize how much you will pay for this love."

THE QUESTIONER

A TRAVELER carried in his hands a mask of disquiet, and his feet were shod with a great longing to reach the Ravine which – so he had been told – could answer his questions. When at last he stood before it, afraid that it might not answer him, he addressed it carefully: "They told·me that anyone overcoming all obstacles and managing to reach you will receive trustworthy answers to the questions that block our progress on the path. If I ask, will you answer?"

The Echo answered: "Ask intelligently and fearlessly for whatever you need. But ask with relevance so that you don't lose what you've already gained."

The traveler asked: "Is it true it's not right to question what someone else has said – or even one's own beliefs or feelings?"

"One verifies when in doubt," answered the Echo, "or when one is not convinced by one's own beliefs."

"I already know that!" exclaimed the questioner. "Can you answer three questions? I find it extraordinary that a Ravine can answer this way."

"I can," replied the Echo. "And this brings the number of answers I've given you to three. But since you're not bright enough to know what you really want, let me give you a final word of advice. It's about time to get rid of your skepticism and lack of faith. Such things block your progress along the path."

A DREAM COME TRUE

ONE fine day, after dreaming so much about love, Little Friend made a sudden decision: "The moment has come," he said to himself, "to see my Queen and to have her with me, not just at nightfall, but also while the sun is in the sky." Full of happiness, he took up his journey and headed toward the distant horizon.

Years of ceaseless searching went by. Finally, one morning, he found her. Time was holding her captive in a cell of loneliness with bars forged by burning tears.

The Queen's plight aroused within him the courage to fight for his Queen in knightly combat. When he had achieved a well-deserved victory, he approached his Queen and said: "My beloved Queen, you have risen from the darkness to see the dawn with different eyes. Look at me! I am the fragment of song you heard in the seashells. Once and for all, open your dawn and spread your face and your wings over my forest.

"I know you'll say I am only your vassal and that you are a Queen, enthroned beyond my reach. But before becoming your slave, I was nobler and freer than the finest knight. In this freedom, I traveled your fields, your vineyards, your rivers, your mountains, your mills – your whole domain. And it was my diamond sword that drove away the tyrant who had shrouded your memory in darkness, hiding those days once so full of happiness."

With new life shining in her eyes, the Queen answered: "I nourished the hope that you would come. I used to see you in my dreams, just as you are now, conquering me to free me, healing my soul's sickness. I beg you, share the visions of your heart with me. But don't offer me what most believe to be real but which is actually ephemeral. Share with me what you've tested and found true, the spark igniting that growth which comes from knowing beauty through the senses. Teach me how to create a new and ever brighter sunrise every day."

DEADLY DISSATISFACTIONS

THERE were once two rebellious Hands who plotted together in secret. One said: "I'm tired of taking orders without ever being asked how I feel." "I feel the same way," said the other, "but I'm even more upset because he makes me work very hard and never gives me a day off. The truth is, our master's a tyrant, and he should get what he deserves."

So the Hands agreed to carry out their revenge. That night, they waited until their master was sound asleep. Then they grabbed him around the neck, crying gleefully: "Now we can do what we want. Yes! At last we'll be free!"

As they were choking their master, the pulse in his brain, beating furiously, shouted: "Stop! Just because you're unhappy, you don't have to destroy everything. If your senseless dissatisfaction is so strong, I can arrange it so you'll be free of his body – but, of course, you won't be able to move."

The Hands were so obsessed that all they heard was the word free, so they readily agreed to be cut off.

From that day on, all the parts of the body, understanding that each was a part of a whole, helped each other and tried to make sure that the new hands didn't feel like stepchildren.

CONCERNING BEAUTY

OVED by the beauty around him, one of the disciples asked his master how he could help others to see and feel such riches.

"What you ask is difficult," answered the old man. "To see and feel beauty outside oneself, one must first be – and feel himself to be – beautiful."

"Master, how do we know if someone is beautiful?" asked the disciple. "And if one isn't beautiful, how does one become so?"

"Beauty is a part of love," the master explained. "It is being great enough to give and humble enough to receive. To help another discover beauty is to open one's spirit to noble and generous ideas. It is removing the egotistic blindfold that covers the mind and tearing off the bandages that shroud the heart."

WINGS

— ◆ —

NTERING the leafy woods, Little Friend saw a bird with a feathery coat of many coffee-colored tones perched nearby, and Little Friend was filled with joy. A black mask framed the bird's eyes, and its wings appeared to be flecked with the reds of daybreak. Seeing its wings stretched outward against the limitless sky as it flew away, Little Friend remembered his childhood when, guided by dreams, his travels knew no boundaries.

Believing that he might recover that feeling of freedom and joy by seeing the bird every day, he decided to capture it. And he did. From then on, his house was filled with happiness and song, and everything he did was accompanied by a smile.

Time passed. One winter morning, Little Friend awoke but did not hear the lovely song with which the bird greeted each new day. Fearing the worst, he rushed over to the cage and found the bird motionless, its vacant gaze fixed on a thin beam of light coming from the window. Taking the bird between his hands and shedding a tear, Little Friend begged the bird to forgive him for enslaving it to his selfish needs. Suddenly Little Friend understood that the bird belonged to everyone and to no one, just like the sun. He realized that imprisoning anything diminishes the beauty of the world.

Full of remorse, Little Friend wanted to let the bird go, but he hesitated, fearing that the bird might die now that winter had arrived. But then he heard a voice say: "If you love me, know the true meaning of my wings. And remember the joy of my freedom."

LITTLE FRIEND
AND THE SOOTHSAYER

———— ◆ ————

AITHFULLY pursuing his quest, Little Friend fell in with a world famous Soothsayer. "What can you tell me about my past, present and future self?" he asked.

Looking at him, the gifted man replied: "Although you're young, I can see centuries flowing through your veins and a star that came with you into the world."

Little Friend answered: "The centuries in my veins represent time, which formed me. But my memory has lost track of them. The star is my life. On its wings I can travel freely."

"Deep inside you I see a road," the Soothsayer continued. "It is trampled by black horses and strewn with the blood of those wounded by brambles and thorns."

As if beginning to remember, Little Friend said: "Yes, the path of my life is littered with refuse."

"Later on," proceeded the old man, "I see born in you an almost calm sea, with clear waters mingling with others full of great green seaweed swaying freely to and fro."

"Yes, I'm almost there now," replied Little Friend.

"On the other side of that sea is a land waiting to be settled," the Soothsayer went on. "It will require work, study, learning, giving. And at the right moment, it will demand that you bow your head as you bend your right knee to the ground."

"That's the place I want to reach," said Little Friend, "where I can be the Space–Time Dawn–Man who, reborn and free, sows stars as he goes."

THE SEA OF THE NORTH

*I*T was said that, on the edge of the Sea of the North, between Silence and the Fountain, there lay a most beautiful land with a vast treasure, guarded by the Wind. It was also said that the Wind would give this treasure to anyone who could conquer it. But no one knew the whereabouts of the Sea of the North, the Fountain or the treasure itself.

A young local man heard these stories. And so he entered the forest on a vision quest. He sought to strengthen his resolve and harden his body before starting on his search for the treasure. Having purified his intentions in this way, he took up his luminous sword and set out toward the north.

Weeks turned into months. Months turned into years. During his search for the Sea, his firm resolve and the readiness of his weapon were the sources of his strength.

One morning, he arrived at a place that looked familiar. It was the very spot where he had begun his search years before. Not knowing which way to turn, he sat down and let the hours slip by. Then Silence appeared and showed him the roads he had traveled, the cities and towns he had passed through and the millions of people who had become a single person with a thousand faces, veiled by the mantle of night.

Days passed. One evening, at twilight, he began to weep. For now he understood. The Sea for which he had searched all these years was within the universe of his own soul. The North was the Fountain which was nourishing him now and which he had reached by his constant searching. He looked at his hand. It was empty. His sword lay at a distance, in among the reeds.

At that moment, the Wind came and started to wipe away his tears. Now a man, he watched the Wind and said: "There was a time when I would have fought you with my sword. But now, without any battle, you have won victory's wreath of laurel."

The Wind, concentrating on drying the man's face, didn't seem to hear him. But when it had finished, it said: "Little Friend, I am the rhythm of your life, with its ups and downs. I have come to pay tribute to you. Although defeated, you have vanquished me. You used no ordinary weapons, but the wisdom to begin to be."

With that, the Wind began to depart for the eternal realms. Seeing the Wind starting to fade away, Little Friend shouted: "Wait! I want to talk with you!"

The Wind was already moving off through the branches. But before disappearing, it slowed for a moment and said: "Little and Great Friend, how I would like to spend more time by your side. But there is much work to do and many more leaves to be blown from their trees."

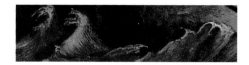

THE FORGE

RESSURED by life's fast pace, I was working my Forge as hard as I could when it said to me: "Little Friend, it is a fact that, if you work me a little, I will forge you a little. It is also true that if you drive me to the extreme, as you do now, you will end up destroying me and yourself."

I replied, "But I feel so pressed by time. There is never enough."

The Forge looked at me with eyes of friendly understanding. "It is not time that pressures us. Look at the seasons – how the flowers bloom and grow steadily from spring into autumn. If time seems short, as you complain, it is because you fail to understand the rhythms of your life. If you were suffering, time would seem long. But now it seems short because you do not know where you are going, and so you ignore the fruits of your work."

Listening thus to my Forge, I sensed her contempt. But feeling secure in myself, I smiled my best smile and reproached her: "Of course I know what I'm doing. I'm on the road to well-being. I will be able to find Love."

Her expression became a bit more friendly as she calmly replied: "You still have much to learn, Little Friend, for well-being is not forged by going to extremes. And as for Love, it is living so that others may exist. This has nothing to do with tomorrow but everything to do with today. Today is the ever-continuing moment that comes and goes in the middle of eternity."

LITTLE FRIEND AND THE ROCK

◆

IN the middle of a grove of trees, with his arms flailing and his eyes turned to the heavens, Little Friend spun round and round with a joy that transported him to ecstasy. He soon lost his balance and fell down on the grass. "What glorious splendor all around!" he cried. "I am truly happy!"

A nearby Rock, feeling uncomfortable with all this, complained: "May I ask why you burden me with your happiness? It is softening me."

Little Friend rolled over on the grass and addressed the Rock lovingly: "It's just that I'm in love with the love that is in everything."

This excited a number of tiny molecules within the Rock. "Are you trying to tell us that you're in love with a woman?"

"I'm only half a person," Little Friend admitted. "So I'm in love with her, my other half. No one is more beautiful, sweeter or better than she."

"Then why isn't she here with you?" asked the Rock.

"Because I am still searching for her through love," replied Little Friend.

The Rock was sarcastic: "Oh, you're still looking for her? Do you really expect to find such a woman – someone so beautiful, so sweet, so tender?"

"Yes, of course," said Little Friend. "I constantly call out for her with the voice of my heart. And I know I will recognize her when I see her."

"He is crazy to believe in love and romance," thought the Rock.

Little Friend reached down and caressed the Rock. Then he danced off into the distance. Every so often he gave a few small jumps of joy.

The Rock returned to its usual passive state, not even noticing that a spider had begun spinning a web in one of its many holes.

SEPARATE PARTS

ONE day, the Feet suddenly announced: "We are the most important parts, for we are the path makers."

Outraged, the Blood and the Veins insisted how essential their work was.

The Hands claimed they were the ones who earned a living.

The Heart boasted of possessing the finest and most sensitive aspects, which gave life to the most sublime emotions.

Other parts, including the Ear, the Mouth and the Eyes, also emphasized their importance.

The Mind didn't bother to speak, knowing that those who boasted obeyed its commands. "Besides," it told itself presumptuously, "I can acquire whatever I want, whenever I want. For I have at my disposal the power of my intellect, of its ideas and imagination."

Thus did the parts of the body keep babbling on, making the place seem like a madhouse.

THE PERFUME SELLER

◆

HE word was out. At last the city had a merchant who offered the most complete selection of perfumes ever available.

After a while, because of the publicity, a rich young lady went to visit the perfume seller. "I want a cologne with a very special fragrance for my husband. I don't like the one he uses, but I don't know what to look for."

After studying her closely, the merchant said: "Madame, there is a fragrance for each personality. It corresponds directly to what one person means to another. I suggest you have a talk with your husband, and then you will know the fragrance you're looking for."

The woman agreed but, before leaving, she asked the merchant about his prices. He replied: "You yourself will set the price for my product," he replied, "but I want you to give that amount to the neediest person you meet."

The young lady was quite surprised by this. But later, when she met an old beggar woman near her home, she gave her the appropriate payment.

Faced with such wonderful generosity, the old woman raised her weary eyes and said: "Bless you, good woman! May God continue giving you the lovely fragrance you have."

As she moved away, the young woman said to herself, "Fragrance? Today, knowing I would visit the perfume seller, I wore none." Deep in thought, she walked on more slowly. Suddenly she turned on her heels and retraced her steps, her face glowing with gratitude. She wanted to thank the perfume seller. But she couldn't find him. She had been his last customer.

THE THIEF OF DREAMS

◆

O N the day of her birth, dawn gave the Queen a vial of crystallized dew, so that she could keep her Vision close at hand.

Having left her adolescent years, the Queen wanted to have a greater Vision. But, in order to obtain it, she stole dreams from the travelers passing through her domain. The travelers – mostly vagabonds – used the Queen's vial to quench their thirst and left the dust of their travels inside the vial. With its contents muddied, the vial began to lose the brightness it had received from the sun. The Vision became sick.

Trying to heal her Vision, the Queen stole even more dreams, and thus the Vision became weaker and weaker.

Then one day, the Vision stammered out in agony: "If you don't act quickly and nourish me with your purity, My Lady, I will surely die. Without me, you will run the risk of traveling to the Land of Nowhere. And there, after traveling through the Vegetable Kingdom, you will be trapped and paralyzed in the Mineral Kingdom, where you will know the hells of immobility."

THOUGHTS

IN the course of time, the Painter's Apprentice realized that he would never become a master. So he decided to devote himself to recording his thoughts. One day, I came across him in the tiny village of Rockport, and he shared some of these thoughts with me:

If you think you come from nowhere, no matter how much you travel, nowhere is where you will end up.

Between lover and loved one the distance is great. The lover opens doors. The loved one expects doors to be opened.

If, on the path, you come across a thorn that makes your bare foot bleed, do not curse it or treat it as an adversary. Our reason for being is to tread the path and, on the path, to learn and, in learning, to find out about flowers and thorns.

If there is a path from God to Man, there is also a path from Man to God.

Don't try to figure out what other people are thinking, because all you'll be doing is thinking your own thoughts.

If you keep thinking – I could have, I knew, I did – there is no today in your house.

In a crowd of people, it isn't enough to merely raise your hand. You must step forward and show your face.

If you have lit a light within you that nourishes even the sun, then there is nothing more you owe to any day.

If you imprison beauty, you will become ugly. The reason you desire her is because she is free.

The greatest tribute you can offer loved ones is not to feel pain and sorrow because they have gone away, and you will never see them again. The greatest tribute is to carry them within you so that they will live forever.

THE CONGRESS

———— ◆ ————

*A*FTER pursuing me relentlessly, the parts of my body finally cornered me. This time there was no escape. They sat me in the witness box. I listened with feigned surprise as each part complained about the work I made it do.

In their hurry to speak, they fell over each other, but Ear got there first: "Little Friend, I am tired of hearing foolish nonsense and all that noise. Before I waste away completely, take me where truth is as vast as the air and every sound is beautiful."

Mouth spoke up in support: "I am sick of talking without rhyme or reason, just to falsely flatter the undeserving. I am tired of telling lies and saying silly things even you can't understand."

The Hands were next: "We are dissatisfied with your daily diet of indifference. It never lets us finish what we start."

The Feet wore a look of sadness and said: "Pity poor us! Aren't we fit to walk on better things than stones and thorns?"

Before speaking, Mind carried me to a vast open space. "The most serious obstacle to my development is the years of accumulated garbage you never get around to throwing out."

Heart then had its say: "I insist that you stop pulling me from side to side, allowing me to live for a few fleeting moments, only to plunge me into many different deaths! I order you to take me once and for all to that place without limits where life is fuller, finer, and always being renewed!"

This mutiny eventually became a congress in which all members could decide their destiny by democratic vote. Since then, Mind and Heart – depending upon the matter under consideration – have governed from their separate chambers. And sometimes, in order to succeed, they have even worked together.

SOMEONE

——— ◆ ———

BATHED in sunlight, Someone once said: "Thank you, Love, for teaching me that life is beautiful and pleasing. Your light has shown me, beyond the rainbow, an infinite world of tenderness where hate, lies and the blackness of emptiness do not exist. I can see things in their true colors, beyond the colors we usually see. Thank you for teaching me the value of the happiness to be found in a smile."

He held a Rose between hands folded in prayer. Hearing him, the Rose murmured: "Loving friend, why do you let the dew of your tears fall on my petals?"

And he, who was just Someone on the face of the earth, replied with a sad smile: "Because Love has taught me to share it with others."

SILLY QUESTIONS
DESERVE NO REPLY

——— ◆ ———

ONE day, in my travels, I came upon a little girl sitting under a leafy tree. Her face rested in her hands, and her arms encircled her drawn-up knees. Moved by this picture, I went up to her and put on my best smile: "Hello, little lady! Can I help you in any way?"

Raising her head gracefully and with a gleam of hope in her eyes she answered with a mixture of joy and sorrow: "I would like to know why adults don't call things by their proper names. Why don't they tell the truth about what they want and what they feel? And why don't they answer when we ask them about all the things that we want to know?"

Silence gripped my tongue.

The beautiful child could see that I didn't know what to do or say. The look she gave me as she got up to leave said: "I'm sorry. I forgot. You're an adult too."

THE SECOND BIRTH

ITTLE FRIEND had nowhere to go, but his feet were still on the path. Then he heard a voice: "By having no goal you paralyze your body, and your journey becomes lifeless." It was the Path ahead which spoke to him, and he reached down to touch it with his hand, asking it why he felt so dead when he had everything he had ever wanted.

"Without a second birth, you live a constant death," replied the Path. Little Friend, thinking the Path was being incoherent, frowned. Seeing Little Friend's expression, the Path smiled because it could read Little Friend's thoughts. Then it said: "Your first birth was your entrance into the world. If you hadn't received warm and caring attention, you would have had your first and – in this case – your only death.

"But you learned to walk. You went through childhood and adolescence. You learned that you were a branch of the tree that gave you life, your family. Up to now, your values have been based on what you've been told at one time or another.

"Your second birth depends on you and you alone. It begins when, using your own intelligence, you decide what it is you really want. Without a second birth, we feel sick and abandoned and faithless. Then this leads us to seek immediate pleasures which quickly fail to satisfy, and to live little lives full of little deaths.

"Giving birth to yourself is discerning what is the highest and most enduring thing of all. If you struggle to achieve this, your prize will be complete independence of thought, belief and action, until you find the light of your own truth and your own inner happiness. Then you will walk in freedom."

FATHER AND SON

ONE day when I was young, I asked my Father:
"Should I be afraid of death?"
"Should you be afraid of life?" was his reply.
And I said: "No, but how should I go about it?"
My Father smiled at me. "Always wear your best smile," he said.

MY NIHILISM AND MY OTHER I

As Night and Silence played with my thoughts, the voice of my Nihilism spoke: "Life is nothing. It always wears the same old clothes to remind us that it ends where it begins. And, though flowers and their perfumes exist, everything passes away, leaving not even a trace of dreams or wakefulness."

My Other I replied: "Life is a momentary flight to the nothingness within eternity. But, through intelligence and character, it is up to me to make of that moment either nothingness or eternity. To feel whole is to make each moment a new and better sunrise, a dawning of love."

"That's not true. What you say is an illusion."

"Of course, life, love and other such things are an illusion, but a grandeur and an abundance exist that give them life. This is the work of the heart."

"The heart? Bah, don't make me laugh!" cried my Nihilism.

And my Other I said: "Every heart is a face wearing a twofold mask of tears and joy. And a heart like yours, without direction, can't know why it weeps when it laughs or when its tears are tears of joy."

SOMETHING

———— ♦ ————

*L*OST in the forest, Little Friend came across an Insect. Aware of its small size and vulnerability, the Insect cried: "Considering my life span, I'm older than you. So treat me with respect."

Further on, Little Friend found himself face-to-face with a beautiful Unicorn. The animal, being a bit nervous, pointed its horn at him and said: "I'm a child, and I've lost my way. Can you tell me how to get back home?"

Next, Little Friend came to a River. As he was gazing at its course, he heard it say: "What you are admiring now has taken centuries to achieve, but I'm only like this when the ice thaws."

Little Friend, looking out into the Universe, pondered its grandeur. As he closed his eyes and saw himself moving through it, he heard these words: "Although I have both beginning and end, my dimensions in space and time are so vast, you'll never explore all of me, even in your dreams."

Then Little Friend remembered he was lost, and a tear larger than usual formed inside him. It spoke with a gentle voice: "Love is each and every phase of living, with no beginning and no end. It is ageless because it is eternal and because it sees nothing as impossible."

THE SHADOW EATER

◆

*S*PEAKING before a busy crowd, a man was saying: "I am a man on the edge of the wind. I work as a shadow eater, just as our friend in the circus is a fire eater. I know how to play their game. I tell them what they need to hear, but sometimes – just sometimes – I am not allowed to tell them everything. Occasionally it's because of love. Other times it's because it would do more harm than good. You've got to be a good diplomat, a builder of good governments. But let's leave politics alone. Although, I must say that at times I can hardly manage to eat the shadows of the cities, the shadow of the economy, the shadows of wars, of the dead. I'm a good shadow eater, and I charge a lot. I demand the thanks of honest and truly grateful eyes, even from those who are full of themselves."

As I watched him, he repeated all of this several times, in several different ways. Then, with lines of bitterness etched on his face, he dropped his hands, which had been cupped around his mouth to form a megaphone. Off he went around the corner, where the wind was howling.

THE TRAVELER

*I*N the course of his travels, a boy became a man, and he continued to travel. He used to say that there was no one quite like him, because he knew all the roads. Everywhere he went, the inhabitants of the places through which he passed were fascinated by the descriptions of his travels, and they began to treat him as a sage.

Once, while walking along a riverbank, he heard a Voice ask: "Little Friend, why do you boast so much?"

Astonished, for he saw no one, he cast his net of words over the water, hoping to catch a reply: "Who's that speaking?"

"I am the waters of a thousand currents," answered the Voice, "and I come from a thousand waterfalls."

"I'm going to get closer in order to hear you better. Don't worry. I know how to get there. I know all the roads." Little Friend plunged into the river and shouted: "Here I am! Now what were you saying?"

But this time the Voice echoed from behind a cloud: "Little Friend, why do you boast so much?"

Little Friend looked up, and his voice followed his gaze: "The road up to you is one I do not know. You will have to come down so I can hear you."

"Is this better?" asked the Voice from inside him.

"No," answered Little Friend, "because I don't know the road into myself."

"If you can neither rise above a mountaintop nor travel into yourself," the Voice challenged, "how can you claim to know all the roads?"

IN SEARCH OF LOVE

*H*AVING heard so much about Love, I decided to seek her out, making Time a witness to my yearning. One day, on an open plain, I met the Wind and asked him about Love. Between murmurs, he answered: "Seek her in pleasure."

For years I fed my senses, searching for Love in pleasure, but the search led me, not into paradise, but into an abyss. Bearing a heavy load of darkness on my back, I approached a Mountain. "Can you tell me where to find Love?" "Seek her in happiness," the Mountain replied. I did as I was told, spending more years in fruitless search.

I traveled on, wrapped in gloom. Finding myself standing before the Ocean, I shouted above its roar: "Surely you must know where Love is. Please tell me. I have lost half my life searching for her. Where can I find her?" And the Ocean answered: "Seek her in knowledge."

I steeped myself in knowledge, and more years passed. I met the Sun, who was so brilliant I had to shield my eyes. When it began to grow dark in my soul, I said: "Brother Sun, during my search for Love, I was told I could find her in pleasure, in happiness and then in knowledge. But I haven't found her. Did Wind, Mountain and Ocean lie to me?"

Shining even more brightly than before, the Sun answered calmly: "No, Little Friend, they didn't lie to you. What happened was you sought pleasure without happiness, happiness without knowledge and knowledge without wisdom."

I stood there speechless, a thousand thoughts dancing to the rhythm of the chaos in my mind. The Sun, seeing me silent and thoughtful, began to set in a blaze of yellow, blue and crimson. While I was gazing into infinity, a tear was born. It trickled slowly down my cheek. When it had almost reached my ear, I heard a soft voice whisper: "Here I am."

THE PAINTING

UTSIDE, snowflakes fell from the icy clouds like bits of cotton. Light from the cabin seemed to change them into little rainbows surrounded by gleaming white halos.

Inside the cabin, a young man and his grandfather sat before an inviting fire, its flames rising and falling in the fireplace. The grandfather was smoking a pipe full of memories while the youth, curious and alert, was examining the painting hanging over the fireplace.

It was a painting of a beautiful nude woman – fragile, simple and pure. At the woman's side sat her shadow. Long black thorns like animal claws protruded from its hands and feet.

Three radiant, transparent spheres, connected by a barely visible thread, hung suspended in front of her body. One sphere enclosed her sexual organs and contained within it the symbol of union between male and female. The second sphere covered her breasts and contained a heart resembling a flower

which was nourished by an iridescent tear. The third sphere, which was around her head, looked like the earth and radiated energy. From the sphere gushed a fountain of thousands of luminous white thorns.

The young woman, her body radiant, was standing with her small bare feet upon a triangle which swung back and forth. The triangle was suspended inside a circle that was swinging in the opposite direction. She was trying to reach a long lever on her right which, if she could only pull it, would stop the swinging and allow her to regain her balance. With her left hand, she was tightly grasping the triangle so she wouldn't fall off. The black thorns of her shadow were flying at her, trying to prick her hands and her feet.

From the sphere around her head poured the brilliant white thorns, falling upon the black thorns and fighting with them in the space around her. The white thorns were beginning to dissolve the black thorns and the blood their wounds had drawn.

When he had finished examining the painting, the young man noticed something at the bottom written in very small letters. The title read: "Two Ends of a Stick."

THE HEART FLOWER

◆

*I*T was somewhere between twilight and nighttime. Downcast and resentful, feeling that life was not worth the effort, Little Friend met a tiny old woman whose hair was as silver as the moon. She was ancient yet ageless, eternal like time, with sad gazelle eyes and a smile that held infinite mysteries in every wrinkle. She was curled up, with her head tucked down in her lap, like a child in the womb. The cold wind blew through every hole in her ragged dress, and Little Friend could see she was hungry.

He spread his cape over her fragile body and gave her his bread and the last of his berries. She ate eagerly and, as she ate, her body was transformed into a light brighter than the sun.

At first, Little Friend was blinded by this miracle. When his sight returned, he saw before him a very beautiful young woman dressed in a queen's flowing robes. Faced with such an incredible vision, Little Friend knelt down, full of humility. "Who are you who reveals herself to me this way?" he asked.

The beautiful woman moved toward him with great majesty. With a voice that filled the surrounding space, she answered: "Don't be afraid, Little Friend, for I am your soul. Until a moment ago I was dying, but now I am reborn."

With a graceful hand, she plucked from her breast a rose, as radiant and magnificent as the light shining around her. With words of fragrant softness, she said: "Take this. Today you have won this flower for your heart. Look after it. It is nourished by love and beauty. And when your mistakes cause it to shed burning tears, please don't curse it."

ON DISCIPLINE

A BOY interrupted the game he was playing to ask his father: "Why is my friend always getting scolded, when you never scold me?"

"Because discipline is imposed only on those who don't do what is right," his father replied.

"But don't you think, after all this time, that my friend must be the way his father wants him to be?"

"My son, if a tree is growing crooked, only a person whose own roots are good can give it the care and attention it needs."

"I don't understand," said the boy.

"What I'm trying to say is that a father who disciplines without being disciplined himself eventually will sow rebellion, not obedience."

BUBBLES

*A*s he sat with his arms around his knees, the young man wandered down memory's path. The wind kept him company at first but later it fell back, unable to pass through colors, things and time to reach the place where a dying man was uttering his last words: "My son, I want to beg your forgiveness for leaving you so desolate . . ."

"Dear father, how can you say such a thing, when you are leaving me such riches?" The old man opened his sad, deep-set eyes. He tried to speak, but his speech was a whisper wrapped in silence.

In the loneliness of mourning his father's death, the young man began to remember. He recalled how he had immersed himself in fleeting pleasures and short-lived friendships. Finally his memories brought him to the present. He looked without seeing, and the wind caught up with him.

It was winter. It was as if everything were held in a bubble by uncertainty's capricious fingers. It was then that a blind man, hearing him speak with compassion about another's misfortune and feeling pity, told him about a sage who could help him.

The young man went to the sage and said: "Venerable master, I have come to you so that the ear of my heart might hear the words that my father wasn't able to speak. I shall pay you well for restoring my heart, whatever the price."

"If you are disposed to pay," the wise man answered, "you will do so – not with riches, but with obedience to my words." After a moment's silence, he continued, with a faraway look in his eyes: "The answer you seek is a short one, but it's like harvesting a fruit that only time can produce. You must plant it, water it and shelter it from the winds of torment you sometimes allow to rule you. If you are sufficiently determined, you will get what you desire. But it won't be I who's the herald for your heart. Your own heart will teach you its reason for being."

Each morning from then on, the sage taught the young man the importance of fruitful work. The evenings, one after another, were for seeing and hearing what was close and even what was far away. It was especially a time for listening to his fellow human beings. At night, the sage made him learn the movements of the heavenly bodies, the language of the stars, the unequaled silent melodies made by small things.

Little by little, the young man began to enter a new universe and to learn how to fill it with peace and happy smiles. Such serenity and bliss sometimes formed a tear, which, expanding in all directions, embraced the farthest corners of the world. And then the young man would humbly say, "Thank you."

Realizing what was happening, the master asked: "Do you now have the answer you have been looking for?"

And the man, now transformed, answered: "Yes. There are no words to express my gratitude."

"You are not indebted to me. You are the one who allowed the light to enter your heart and reveal the path of life. It is a path that has always been where you see it now. But you saw it, as most still do, through shadows within a bubble that did not allow your wings to spread. You can go now, but first I want to hear your new voice."

The man looked up, and his calm, harmonious voice seemed to extend to the far horizon: "Every moment is a beginning and an end, immense and fruitful. At the same time, such moments must be sown and helped to grow, to ripen, in order to understand the value they have. They are the only true food of life, and they can never be duplicated."

THE COMPLAINER

HERE was once a man who went from town to town. He considered himself a very learned fellow. Besides reading many books, he had also arranged a system for classifying the people he met.

While sitting in the shade of a tree one day, he began to remember the story of his life. "Poor humanity!" he said to himself, "Poor man – at once both genius and lunatic. He's like a door that can't be opened because it's rusted shut with lies and hate. Poor rational animal, walking on the edge of each moment, with two feet, three, four or sometimes none. Poor flower of humanity, you've become a thorn that spills torrents of blood over deserts that you've created in yourself."

He was still complaining when a lovely fruit fell at his feet. He picked it up, saying: "Poor thing, falling to your death from such a great height!"

And the Fruit answered: "Little Friend, the right to speak about the many forms of poverty belongs to those who have tried to do something about it. By talking and thinking without acting, as you do, you are an example of the cause of this poverty which you talk about so much. Like so many others, you hide behind your complaints. As for me, how little you know, if you don't understand that every twilight heralds a dawn."

SEEDS
— ◆ —

ONCE a teacher handed out seeds to his pupils for planting and growing. Some time later, he asked his three most outstanding students what they had learned and what they had found most satisfying.

"I learned that my seed could flower and develop into a fruit," said the first. "My satisfaction is in learning that."

The second student spoke next: "I learned that, with attention, care and perseverance, small things can become large and useful. My satisfaction is in adding a good grade to my school record."

"I began to learn how to take care of someone who, for the moment, was smaller than myself," answered the third student. "My satisfaction is in realizing that the greatest pleasure and delight is not to be found in what we give of ourselves, but in what we receive from something that has flourished through our care."

LIFE

— ◆ —

IFE is death," said the old man. "Life is fun," declared the teenager. "Life is children," said the mother. "Life is suffering," groaned the penitent. "Life is money," said the rich man; "Pleasure," said the hedonist; "Playing games," said the child; "The sea," said the sailor; "God," said the priest.

And then they asked: "What's your opinion, Little Friend?"

Little Friend seemed to be walking over a bridge that began in the gaze of his eye and ended on the horizon. He turned back slowly from his contemplation of infinity. His eyes shone with a peculiar brilliance as he began to speak in the gentle tones of prayer: "Life is a time in space, a path which is, in every moment, a constant dying and rebirth."

Then Little Friend continued his journey across the bridge of his vision to that place where, in a sublime moment, sea and sky, day and night are made one.

HOPE AND FAITH

——— ◆ ———

IME fell upon the left hand, and it began to age and then wither away. With sisterly concern, the right hand set out in quest of an elixir that would restore the left hand's youth but, alas, she grew just as old in the process. The legs also tried but met the same fate.

Little by little, the body grew weaker and weaker. But when Hope seemed about to die, the voice of Faith declared: "These lesser parts don't matter. They will recover, if you take care of your heart."

SHADOWS

ONCE upon a time, a wise man was surrounded by his disciples. One of them asked: "As we travel our paths, Master, should we keep our shadow ahead as a guide or behind as a follower? Which is better?"

And the wise man answered: "If someone is small – not physically small, but small because he is full of bitterness – then his shadow will be even smaller. But neither of the shadows you mentioned is better than the other. One drags you along, and the other holds you back." Gravely, he added: "Your shadow is an absence and, as such, should be assigned to obscurity."

"How should I do that, Master?" asked the disciple.

"Regardless of time or circumstances," the wise man replied, "make sure the sun is always directly above you. Then neither sham nor shadow can exist."

THE CITY OF ETERNAL LIGHT

ONE day, his face lit by a brilliant smile, Little Friend was musing: "I know, because I've wanted it fiercely for so long, that I will find the city of my dreams in which will be the peace I've been seeking. Although her days will be marked by sun and moon, there will be no darkness, because she is called The City of Eternal Light. There will be neither sound nor silence. Her fullness will allow me to exist and to be. Then I will know that I have reached my final destination."

His quest went on for years and years, until one very ordinary day turned out to be the most special day of his life. Slowly, almost not believing it could be true, he found himself approaching the city for which he had yearned.

As he drew near, Little Friend heard a voice that came from everywhere and nowhere: "The road you have traveled to get here has been hard. But that doesn't give you the right to enter. In front of you is a door, and behind it are four more. The key to opening each door will be the good deeds you can proclaim."

In front of each of the five doors, Little Friend recited a verse.

1

I have peered beyond the border of the heavens.
I have been to each and every star.
Far beyond the confines of the planets,
Accompanied only by my shadow,
I have walked anew in footprints from my past.

2

Many times I have traveled in God's Heaven,
And have also spent some time in Satan's Hell.
I have seen that both of these are really equal,
When looked at
From their still and silent centers.

3

I have seen the Earth vomit from its entrails,
A brutal fire, gushing from its volcanos.
And I have also seen it bleeding from all the many wars,
In which we become more brutal than the beasts;
These are the final weavings of a deadly spider's web.

4

I have traveled far, and all the paths I've taken,
Have shown to me exactly the same roads,
Familiar situations, the same people,
In precisely that one Light
Which has always made me shiver.

5

I have seen the Soul, which is the dawn within our Spirit,
Which we have made a vagrant ghostly Shadow.
I even know the meaning of all the secret teachings,
And after all of this, I say
Without Love nothing matters.

THE BALANCE

◆

ONCE upon a time, Owl sat perched on a
branch, with Day on one side and Night on
the other.

"There are people," said Owl, "who think that life is
made of tears, that everything around them is negative
and that love is a utopian dream."

"I have seen that this is so," said Night.

"There are people," Owl continued, "who think that
life is loving, living and striving to advance each day,
displaying a smile like a banner as they journey through
life with a light in their hearts."

And Day said: "I have seen that this is so."

THE ENAMORED HEART

AT a gathering of hearts, one stood out from all the rest because of the intensity of his beauty and radiance.

"Let him who sheds tears of love step forward!" he commanded. "What? Is no one coming forward? Does no one have eyes soft with tears? No one! Bless you, my fellow Hearts. For such tears burn fiercer than fire, and in their waters – the salt waters from all the oceans – are cruel fingers which slowly choke and drown you."

THE TALKERS

⸻ ◆ ⸻

*L*ITTLE FRIEND bumped into a signpost pointing to The Mountain of Talkers. He made his way there and found that it was like a pyramid with various levels where different groups of people had gathered.

At the foot of the mountain, a jostling crowd was arguing with the rocks and bushes. Their arguments always ended with the same words: "Bah! The rocks and bushes always win!"

On the next level, people were using mirrors to argue with themselves. When they won, they smiled and stroked the image reflected in their mirrors. When they lost, they immediately turned their mirrors over.

The level above had fewer people, all of whom were walking around absorbed in their own thoughts. Suddenly they would pause, stand still for a moment, then make a triumphant gesture, as if they had just understood something. Then they would mumble to themselves with great satisfaction.

The few people on the fourth level were either looking up at the sky or all around at nature in its many forms. From time to time, their faces would light up and, indulging in some personal revelation, they would coo and murmur sounds of private rapture.

At the top of the mountain, a mere handful of people sat meditating. Their faces reflected an inner radiance and, when asked what they were doing, none seemed to hear the question.

With a smile, partly inspired by all these people and the fullness of the atmosphere, Little Friend remembered the advice of those he had met at the bottom of the mountain: "Pay no attention to those at the very top. They're crazy. They think they're talking to God."

ON REALLY LIVING

⸻ ◆ ⸻

One night when grief turned into emptiness, Little Friend became a Question which assumed the following shape:

Day After Day
we
a
r
e
held
i
n
Life's but hands
w
h
e
n
d
o
w
e
hold life in our hands?

Unnoticed, a white Light came in through the window, amused itself zigzagging through the letters and then said: "Happiness and sadness are the two extremes that give life its fullness."

Little Friend's shape turned into a request:

I wish to Live
from
the
Other Extreme
t
e
l
l
Me how I while can do so
i
e
k
e
e
p
i
n
g
happiness beside me?

Playing with the new letters, the Light replied: "First you must remove that mask of fear from your Heart. Give it wings so it can soar into the land of your dreams.

In return, your Heart will lead you to the Valley of Hope where the Dawn, which is sleeping within you, will awaken and teach you not to worry about time and space. Wherever you are, you are part of the universe. You will then become a loving person, carrying your own riches and blessings within you wherever you go. Then you will find indescribable peace and pure love."

THE MOURNERS

A MASTER and his disciple walked by a cemetery under the noonday sun. Inside, there were two mourners, each in front of a different grave. One was loudly lamenting and rending his garments; the other was weeping silently.

Moved by the sight of the first man, the disciple could only say: "How much he must have loved his dear one!"

"That's certainly true," the master agreed, "but the cause of his suffering today is that he didn't express his love yesterday."

"Master," asked the Little Friend, "if one's suffering is immense because one loved greatly, does this mean the other mourner didn't really love, doesn't feel lonely and therefore is suffering less?"

"It's true that the more we feel that something belongs to us, the more its loss makes us suffer," answered the master. "But if you look closely, you will realize that, while one tears his clothes on the outside, the other tears himself on the inside.

"The first, by not having given all his love, is like a child, who can only take. Because of this, he suffers remorse and wonders who will fill his needs. He'll end up settling for anything he thinks might console him.

"The second, weeping silently, has lost not just a protector, but a true companion. That means that a part of himself – perhaps the best part – died with his friend. But look closely at him again. His face is shining with gratitude, as if to say 'I love you and carry you inside me. There will never be anyone who can take your place.'"

THE MIRROR

◆

ONE day, I proudly looked at myself in the Mirror. I was wearing a laurel wreath. In my vanity, I asked what victory had earned this prize, and the Mirror told me it was the reward for being so self-assured.

Another day when I looked in the Mirror, there was no laurel wreath. There wasn't even an image. Just the Mirror with its frame of silence. After a very long time, the Silence began to speak haltingly: "Feeling secure is fine, so long as you know in advance that the journey will take you across oceans, over mountains, and through deserts. If you are prepared, you can overcome all storms and obstacles. But someone like you, who takes no precautions and thinks he's always in control, doesn't even know that his boat is at sea."

A DROP OF CRYSTAL
AND THE SUN

SOMETIMES because of bad choices and other times because of his conditioning, Little Friend had, in the course of his travels, accumulated a strange collection of years in all manner of colors, shapes and sizes. As he was reflecting on them one day, they began to merge inside him and, after appearing to pass through a pure white filter, they emerged at the other end in the shape of a trembling crystal tear about to fall.

All at once his face came back to life, his ears popped and the painful smothering silence vanished. Little Friend suddenly knew how to gently caress things without trying to possess them and how to perceive their hidden fragrance. Everything he tasted was like nectar. His body was full of comfort and joy. Before, it had been as though he were walking at the bottom of the sea. Now he moved freely. He acquired a noble, but simple bearing. This allowed him to move with ease through the small worlds and vast universes he encountered, greeting everything with love.

Little Friend was walking one afternoon when the Sun, half hidden behind some dark clouds, said: "Lately, a sweet scent has been rising from your breast. It has even reached me up here. May I travel along with you?" Little Friend nodded. The Sun came out from behind the clouds and walked by his side, murmuring to itself: "How satisfying it is to walk with an equal."

And as they went on together, the light of the Sun shone through Little Friend's crystal drop, painting the whole world with seven beautiful, vivid colors.

THE MENDER OF MASKS

LITTLE FRIEND ran through the last of the forest to meet the Mender of Masks. "At last," he panted, "I've caught up to you. I badly need your help."

The Mender of Masks, who clearly didn't wear a mask himself, told Little Friend to lie down, go to sleep and dream. While Little Friend was dreaming, the Mender peeled off his mask. He examined it carefully, but he found nothing wrong with it. So he put it back on Little Friend.

When he awoke, Little Friend asked: "Can I now walk with the sun, sing with the birds, enjoy life and travel its path without fear?"

"Indeed, you can," answered the Mender of Masks.

And Little Friend left, a brand new smile lighting his face.

THE UNHAPPY
HAPPINESS SALESMAN

THERE once was a man who sold happiness, but who was himself unhappy. And he went on being unhappy, until the day he bought some of his own merchandise.

THE ELIXIR OF LIFE

A master asked of one of his most faithful followers why he always listened to him with such devotion.

"What I learn from you makes me what I am," the disciple replied. "I often wonder how you began to obtain wisdom. Will you tell us?"

"It was a long time ago," the master said, smiling at the recollection. "I was obsessed with finding a wise woman, who lived in a house on top of a very special hill, months of travel away. Paying no attention to the poor clothing of the woman who welcomed me, I told her, with some passion, of my desire to acquire wisdom.

"Calmly, giving no hint of immaturity, she asked me if I was ready to receive such a treasure, for it would involve time and responsibility.

"Glowing with happiness, I assured her that I was ready. If that was so, she said, I should go to a nearby town. At the address she gave me, I should ask for the owner and tell him I had been sent to collect the vial containing the elixir of life. I should then return to her with this special vial.

"Following her instructions, I reached the town and the residence I was seeking. I asked the servants for their master but, hearing the reason for my visit, they merely laughed. Only after repeatedly knocking at the big front door, could I get them to take me to the owner. He was entertaining guests.

"I explained why I was there. In good humor, he declared it an amusing and entertaining joke. Then, offering me a few coins, he said I could leave.

"I tried to point out that no joke was intended, but he kept asking me to leave. Quite earnestly, I told him I couldn't go anywhere until he gave me the flask containing the elixir of wisdom. My persistence earned me a thrashing from his servants, who then tossed me into the street.

"Painfully, I went back to tell the wise woman what had happened. This time, a dignified, well-dressed lady welcomed me. Tending my wounds, she asked how I had come by them. When I recounted the story, she gave an understanding smile and said to herself: 'Well, my servant girl certainly seems to be learning.'

"Stupefied, I interrupted: 'Was that the servant girl I saw when I came to the house before? She certainly fooled me!'"

"'Yes, she's the servant,' the wise woman confirmed, 'but you weren't fooled. You came for wisdom, and you learned the first truth. Always doubt what people tell you, unless it's logical and reasonable. And, more importantly, always be suspicious when someone tells you a treasure can be easily acquired.'"

BELONGINGS

⸺ ◆ ⸺

STRUGGLING along under a dark cloud, Little Friend kept falling down. His veins were full of the liquor of emptiness, and he was drunk with loneliness. After one fall, he stayed where he was, lamenting his tragedy.

The Wind blew around him and heard his weeping and moaning. "What have I done to deserve this? Why am I reduced every day to nothing, abandoned by the love that belongs to me?"

"Little Friend," said the Rain running down his face, "your own behavior is making you feel this nothingness. Look at yourself! Now tell me – does love mean treating yourself like this?"

Looking at himself, Little Friend slowly bowed his head and muttered: "No, I don't think so."

"How," demanded the Rain, "can you ask for something to belong to you if you don't belong to yourself?"

THE APPRENTICE

*I*NSPIRED by some paintings on display at the Metropolitan Museum, Little Friend decided to seek out the artist. He spent months searching for his house. The stars, like fireflies, lit his nighttime travels.

His determined searching was finally rewarded. "Master," he said reverently, "I have come to humbly ask you to teach me about line, color and form. Show me the path that your brush has found to those hidden valleys of the imagination.

"Please be generous and show me those amazing roads leading to the Kingdom of Light which, in our lust for power, we have allowed to become overgrown with weeds, losing the light in our faces and the protection of good fortune.

"Please consider me worthy to share your understanding of that land where dreams and poetry go hand in hand. I know that hospitality reigns there, that solitude is not loneliness, that peace is to be found there, as well as happiness and a constant song of praise to life. Show me this ancient human realm to which we can no longer fly because our wings have withered away.

"Master, let your wisdom be my guide. I promise I will learn what freedom is." Listening to all this, the master remembered what he'd been told when he had first arrived there as an apprentice himself years before. He repeated those same words to Little Friend: "Your freedom and love are greater than anything my brush can give you. But, if you want, you are welcome here in my house. I make only one request – that you be the one to teach me."

PROCLAIMING
ONE'S OWN TRUTH

◆

HERE was once a person who said evil didn't exist. He argued that, because there was no evil in nature, human beings – nature's masterpiece – couldn't possibly be evil.

With his smile serving as his scepter and peace as his guide, he went from town to town, proclaiming his truth. He got insults and jeers in return. And he cried in his heart when he saw the world still filled with tyranny, theft, hate, envy and the bloodshed of countless years. His smile turned to sorrow. The tears on his face were like the spray of the ocean. But he kept going because he believed that his insight was real knowledge and therefore truth.

One day, when he was already an old man, he climbed to the top of a mountain. From there he could see the far-off peoples of the earth. When weeks went by and he did not return to civilization, those who had been his disciples became very worried. They searched for him, but in vain.

All they found on the mountain summit was a flowering bush, which gave off a great fragrance. Its flowers had petals like red velvet, covered with shimmering dewdrops as if they were tearful eyes looking toward the four corners of the earth. The disciples had never before seen such a majestic piece of nature. The name they gave the flower was Rose.

THE LITTLE BLUE FLAME

◆

A YOUNG boy, running through valleys and over tree-covered hills, felt something inside him which made him overflow with joy. He wondered why this almost painful happiness always overtook him when he was surrounded by trees. Not knowing the answer, he turned to his grandfather, who was gazing at the wind as it moved through the leaves and branches of the trees.

Smiling, his grandfather told him that the happiness he felt was caused by the Little Blue Flame. Not having told his grandson this story, he began: "Long ago in a faraway place was the Kingdom of Blazing Fires. One day a great freeze came down from the North, and the Kingdom's inhabitants began to be extinguished, one by one.

"Realizing that the catastrophe would be total, the King and Queen decided they must save their three young daughters, three Little Flames – one Red, one Yellow and the youngest one, Blue. They built them three tiny ships, which they loaded with incense to keep the little flames from dying out. Seeing them off, they said: 'Dearest daughters, to save you, we must send you to Earth. Each of you has special gifts, in addition to the normal warmth that gives your lives direction. From now on, that lovely planet will be your home. Show your gratitude by offering its people the special gifts you possess.'

"But the royal parents didn't know their daughters very well. When they reached Earth, Red Flame and Yellow Flame stole their little sister's incense and ran off.

"Red Flame, because she was wicked, refused to share her gifts of strength and endurance in the face of misfortune. Hate and vengeance thus entered the world, although noble people didn't surrender to them.

"Yellow Flame was supposed to offer her gifts of alertness and knowing when to act. But, like her older sister, she devoted herself to evil. Moreover, she was sick with dissatisfaction, and she transmitted this attitude to apathetic people whom she infected with envy. This envy made them ambitious, which resulted in a lack of intelligence, making them unable to distinguish good from evil or justice from injustice.

"Because her sisters had stolen her incense so that they could live, Little Blue Flame grew smaller every day. She became so weak that finally only a few brief sparks remained. She was almost at the point of extinction, when she suddenly remembered what her dear parents had told her – to offer her gifts to the people on Earth. Making one last tremendous effort, she succeeded in entering the surrounding trees. With the passing of centuries and the birth of more trees, the Little Blue Flame multiplied. Now she inhabits every tree on Earth. Her mission is to help people have strength and confidence in themselves.

"That," concluded the young boy's grandfather, "is why you have this feeling of great joy throbbing in your breast. When you are among the trees, the Little Blue Flame enters you."

THE SOUL SURGEON

*L*ITTLE FRIEND was admitted to the hospital in great pain. They decided that his sickness was caused by excessive skepticism and sadness. He was rushed to the emergency room, where he underwent major surgery.

During his convalescence, Little Friend got to know the surgeon, and he asked him for details about his operation. The surgeon produced a flask containing musical notes, which were distorted and decayed. He said he had removed these notes and had replaced them with the silences needed for harmony in the soul.

When the surgeon added that he had been able to repair some other notes, Little Friend asked him what materials he had used to repair them. The doctor showed him a crystal jewel box containing shining rainbow threads, sunset-colored dyes and fragments of dreams and visions.

THE LOVER OF THE MOON

HE determined Opener of Paths was working one day without his staff, which also served as his torch, when he suddenly found himself engulfed by the night. He was driven like a light looking for its source and thus became a Lover of the Moon.

With the help of her silver light, his efforts to open up paths were crowned with success. But when there was no Moon, no light shining down like pillars supporting the heavens, he couldn't do his work, even if the sky was like a starry mantle.

On one occasion, while waiting for his Moon, he saw her appear in the daytime sky. From then on, he no longer opened paths only at night.

THE LITTLE BEAR

TARING into space and daydreaming, Little Friend noticed at the edge of his vision that he was being watched by a Little Bear.

Still in his dreamy state, Little Friend said with a lazy smile: "Hello, Little Bear. With your small paws outstretched like that, it's as if you want to hug me – thank you. Thank you so much for your lovely smile and for the light in your eyes. They're like an oasis of peace."

Little Friend became introspective and sad. "The truth is," he said to himself, "I don't really like your furry coat, which is dark like my own dark body. But I've always wanted to be like you, with a smile like yours and with eyes like yours which contain no evil. And those arms! I'd like to be able to reach out with my own arms and hug the whole world." Interrupted by sobs, he cried: "Oh, Little Bear, how I would like to be you, able to bring happiness to some child."

"Come here," said the Little Bear. "Hug me."

VOICES

— ◆ —

I WAS wandering aimlessly among the sunlight and shadows of an unknown land, when Echo said to me: "Open your ears, listen, hear."

Later, a luminous Beam, shining through the trees and branches, stopped me: "Open your eyes, look, see."

Wind, making waves in the trees, had its turn: "Walk, fly, feel."

Then my eyes were drawn to a Flower, whose fragrance spoke into my ear: "Be friendly, give freely of your own special perfume."

A nearby Bird landed on my shoulder and warbled: "Spread your wings, be free, be your own master."

Intrigued by these commands, I continued on my way. On the road, I met a Worm dragging itself along with great difficulty. Noticing me, it addressed me in a tiny voice: "Know yourself, respect the small, be big."

Looking up, I saw a Mountain and was shaken by the power of its voice: "Be great, be a fountain, be a source of waterfalls."

Then a Cloud's shadow covered me and said: "Be graceful, transparent, fertile."

I went on walking, keeping pace with the River that flowed alongside. "Look at me and learn," it said. "You can't go back. Stagnation is death. To live is to go forward."

River took me to Sea, whose voice was like sensuous music keeping time with the rhythm of its foamy waves: "Be powerful, majestic, unconquerable."

Coming from far off, where Sea and Sky meet, I heard: "Be spacious, serene, clear."

Almost unannounced, Night fell and, speaking from its shadows, said: "Learn from the darkness, from all stages and cycles. Watch over your dreams."

Above me – a compass for my eyes – a Star twinkled: "Be a lofty example, be brilliant, be shining."

Accompanied by Sea, Sky, Star and Night, Earth gave birth to Sun, who said: "Be light at its zenith, shine on everything around you."

I felt ecstatic, adventurous. Then I heard the voice of Love: "Let me be your guide, love yourself, love everything."

Suddenly, without warning, a loud voice yelled: "That's enough for today, Little Friend. Wake up and get going!"

Annoyed, I demanded: "And who are you to interrupt this way?"

The Voice replied: "I am your Conscience."

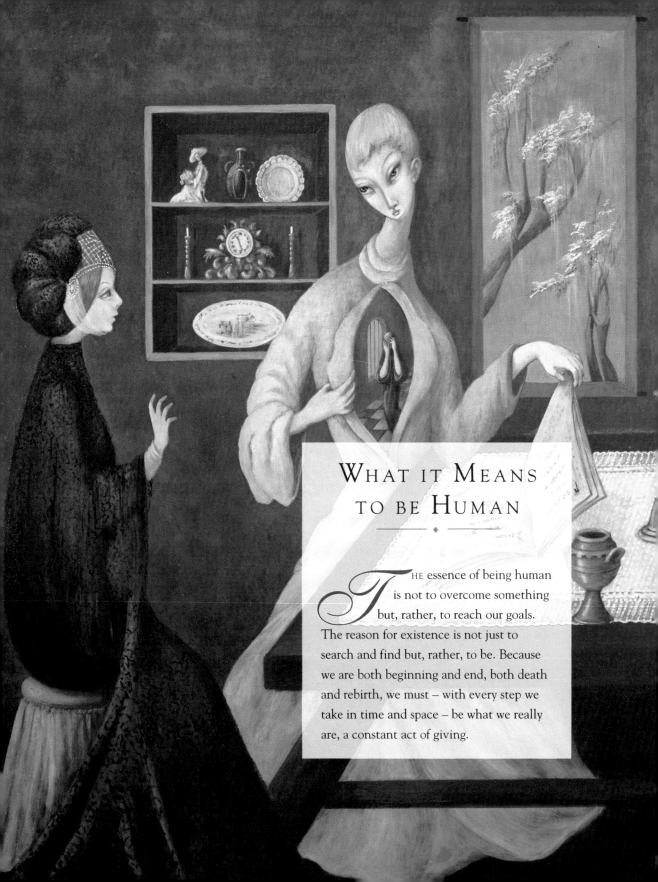

WHAT IT MEANS TO BE HUMAN

THE essence of being human is not to overcome something but, rather, to reach our goals. The reason for existence is not just to search and find but, rather, to be. Because we are both beginning and end, both death and rebirth, we must – with every step we take in time and space – be what we really are, a constant act of giving.

KINGDOMS

——— ♦ ———

*S*ITTING there uncomfortable and dissatisfied, I was watching the river of my life flow by when I thought I saw, beneath the turbulent waters, something shiny lying on the riverbed. When I reached in to get it, the water turned into fire. The shiny object, wanting to spare me excruciating pain, detained me: "There are fires that can burn and consume you but, if you are strong, you will succeed in putting them out." Gritting my teeth, I reached to the bottom of the stream and retrieved my Heart.

I talked to my Heart, and I told it how I longed to love, but without being wounded anymore.

"That's not loving. Loving is giving – giving of yourself without any conditions, with no regard for anything unpleasant that may occur."

"Giving of myself has been my big mistake," I said. "People confuse kindness with stupidity and love with humiliation. And then they think me small and unimportant."

"Which is more important," my Heart asked, "what others see in you or what you know yourself to be? Is it your fault they feel the way they do? Besides, why do you want people to be the way you think they should be? Each person, every thing belongs to a Kingdom. So if you don't think you're in the right place, then spread your wings and fly to the Kingdom where you belong."

AN ANSWER FROM A DREAM

*L*ITTLE FRIEND was sitting in a chair in his garden, unaware of the beauty all around him. "Why do I feel so unhappy?" he asked himself. "I'm young, rich, admired and in good health." He kept asking himself this question over and over until he fell asleep and had the following dream.

It was dawn. The night's foggy mist paled, looking like a cotton sheet flapping in the wind, then slowly faded away. Flocks of birds immediately began to sing. Slowly but surely the whole world came alive. Each and every thing, every creature began to wake up, taking off the dark gown of night and donning the brilliantly colored robe offered by the Sun.

Little Friend was a lazy sun who, yawning and stretching, grumbled: "Oh my, here comes another day. I guess I have to get up and be on my way." Listlessly he arose and traveled across the sky until he reached high noon, where he stood still for a moment. Looking down, he saw an old man surrounded by young people, all listening attentively, except for one who was absorbed in himself. Looking more closely, Little Friend was shocked to see that the inattentive one was himself. This particular student suddenly interrupted the others.

"Master, can you tell me how I can find happiness?"

"Happiness can be found in many ways. One way is to pursue it arduously, with passionate desire. But there is another way which is very simple and basic and, without it, no true happiness can be found. It is being able to feel the great joy of being alive."

And at that moment, Little Friend woke up.

DESTINY

—— ◆ ——

ONCE upon a time there was a little boy whose treasure was a flower. But as time passed, the flower began to wilt, losing its color and scent. "Are you sick, Little Flower?" the boy asked sadly.

The Flower half opened her eyes and barely managed to answer: "I'm not sick, my gentle guardian. It's just that I have reached the end of my destiny and have to say goodbye. Thank you for taking such good care of me."

Worried, the little boy ran home. "Grandad," he cried, "does destiny mean to die?"

"No, my son," the old man smiled, "destiny means to grow."

Still not satisfied, the boy asked: "And do you know where destiny will lead me?"

"This is something only you will be able to discover." Seeing that the boy still didn't understand, the old man smiled, sat him on his knee and said: "I'll explain by telling you a story that took place at the very beginning of time. Listen closely.

"One day a man was out walking when he was confronted by a Wall which said: 'Stop, Little Friend. I am your destiny! This is as far as you can go.' But Little Friend turned himself into a mouse and slipped through a tiny hole in the wall. He went on, guided by self-confidence and his heart.

"Later, he found himself confronted by a River as big and as wide as the sea. It also said: 'Stop, Little Friend. I am your destiny! This is as far as you can go.' But Little Friend turned himself into a fish and swam to the farther shore, where he followed the path laid out for him by the sun.

"Then one day he had to stop suddenly because a deep, dark Abyss lay at his feet. It also said: 'Stop, Little Friend! I am your destiny! This is as far as you can go.' But Little Friend turned himself into a bird, spread his wings and rode the wind to the other side, where he continued on his journey.

"Some time later, he encountered a Valley as long and as broad as the horizon, fertile with delicious fruits, beautiful flowers, majestic mountains, lakes and waterfalls. 'Stop, Little Friend,' said the Valley, 'I am your destiny.'

"And the Little Friend replied: 'At last! How I welcome you!'"

THE LOAFER

WHILE in a village, Little Friend got to know a man who worked harder than anyone he had ever known. Intrigued by this exceptional fellow, he asked him: "Why, good man, do you work with such effort and persistence?"

Wiping his brow, the man smiled and answered: "Because I am a Loafer and very lazy." Realizing that Little Friend didn't understand this contradiction, he explained: "The truth is I really am lazy, but I like to live very well. So, to dedicate myself to loafing, I work very hard part of the time. Then I can spend the rest of my time lying around, but with everything I need and want at hand."

BLUE FIREFLIES

———— ◆ ————

ITH dusk entering his eyes, Little Friend wondered: "What can compare with the blue of the sea for making one feel calm, with the blue of the sky for seeing the earth, with the blue of a flower for savoring its scent, with the blue of a bird for traveling light?

"What is there like the blue of a rainbow for letting one feel rain, the blue of endless space for gazing into the distance, the blue of an eye for veiling a dream?

"What is there like the blue of the dawn, which gives birth to each day; the blue of a cloud, which waters the fields; the blue of the night, which brings serenity?

"Oh, who will give me the blue light of peace, beauty and love?"

Sparkling blue stars began to emerge from the night in Little Friend's eyes. A firefly, who had been listening, approached and said: "Please let me stay in your garden, Little Friend, and feed my small light from yours, so beautiful and blue."

THE POET

— ◆ —

*I*N a classroom of the School of Life, several students were discussing their ideas about man as an individual. When it was his turn to speak, the most reserved among them said, with some reluctance: "Far beyond where most people see, the Poet sees. Far beyond pain, far beyond the place where hope seems to have died, stands the Poet. Far beyond everything and nothing, far beyond happiness and the metaphysical, lives the Poet. He has the cure for everything, and he can change water to silver, dew to diamonds. He turns the ocean into a puddle, a tear into the sea. He gives life to a stone, making it roll and suffer, just like himself. Far beyond the distant, fleeting stars, way beyond the universe, the Poet lives with God.

"Each of us is a Poet. We only need to shake off our daily trappings and let the Sun come in, to understand that we are here, like the smallest rock, naked and quiet, so that we can become human. So that we can become poets."

When he was finished, some students were silent, some smiled and others made fun of him.

The class continued, and the most articulate were asked to comment on the different forms of government. When the shy student was called on to speak, he claimed he was at a loss for words.

The class ended for the day and his classmates started to leave, but Little Friend remained behind to correct some notes. About to leave, he noticed on the reticent student's desk a sheet of paper on which the following was written:

"I'm not going to raise my hand and talk about isms. No, I'm not going to do it! I'm a small, quiet person, whose only light casts my shadow, whose only hunger is within my breast, whose only sweat is my tears. No, I'm not going to talk about isms. I come from a country without a name, and the moment I arrived here, I began my journey back home. I mean, from time immemorial I've been the memory of everything forgotten. I can't die because I'm a seed, and I'm forgotten because I know nothing. As I told you, I'm small and quiet, like the earth's dust. I'm like a star, naked, cold and still, alone in the mantle of the night, which awaits me without *isms*."

BEAUTY AND THORNS

———— ◆ ————

MARVELING at a Rose, Little Friend was overcome with joy and plucked her. Her thorns pricked his finger, and his cry of pain awakened the sleeping Flower. Seeing herself held captive, she said softly: "Why do you complain, Lover of Beauty? Was it not you alone who chose to take me in your hands?"

THE CROW AND THE FARMER

———— ◆ ————

TWO young Crows were complaining bitterly up in a treetop: "It's not fair! This farmer has thousands of ears of corn, but he won't let us have even a few – not without running the risk of finding ourselves in the sights of his shotgun!"

Then the Crows heard about a man who worked miracles. They approached him and asked him to turn one of them into a farmer. This accomplished, the new Farmer agreed to let the remaining Crow have all the corn he wanted.

Time passed. The Farmer plowed, sowed, watered his seeds and watched his crop growing ready for harvest – an event in which the Crow was eager to share.

The Crow showed up at harvest time, delighted he could now do what he had never done before – eat freely of the corn. Instead, he was greeted with several warning gunshots.

"Brother, it's me!" cried the Crow. "Don't you recognize me?"

His brother, the Farmer, approached. "Of course I recognize you! If you don't get out of here, you won't live to tell the tale."

"That's not fair!" exclaimed the Crow. "Don't you remember our deal?"

"Of course I remember it! But it seems even more unfair to me that, after I've worked so hard, you should calmly fly in to help yourself to the fruits of my labor."

THE CLOUD

A s I had done so many times before, I turned my eyes towards the setting sun. Out of the corner of my eye I noticed a tiny Cloud. As I was looking at her, the Cloud asked: "Don't you get tired of staring at me?"

"No, I don't."

A few moments later, she said: "Don't you have anything better to do than to stand there looking at me?"

"No, actually, I don't."

"For a human being, you're not very smart," the Cloud exclaimed angrily. "Your time on earth is short, and all you do is waste it!"

"I'm not wasting it."

The Cloud didn't hear me. The wind had jerked her away like a puppet on a string. Behind where she had been, the Sun was setting and, stretching wide its brilliant arms, it invited me to join its fiery celebration.

FAITH AND HUMANITY

O NE day, during his travels, Little Friend came across someone even smaller than he was. He did what he could for him.

A Magpie, who was watching, just couldn't stop laughing. "Do you still have faith in the likes of him?" he squawked.

"If I stopped having faith in people," Little Friend replied, "I would cease to exist."

MUTUALITY

——— ◆ ———

A ROSE and a Bush were talking. "Each time you bloom, you get cut down," the Bush objected. "I can't understand why you're happy. Don't you realize that those who cut you only care about the pleasure they get from putting you in a vase?"

"Satisfying their desires makes them happy, I know," the Rose replied. "But I'm even happier, and my pleasure is greater. Because they allow me to fulfill my purpose – to bring happiness to those who really need it."

THEN AND NOW

——— ◆ ———

L ONG ago, I was a rock which mighty, incessant waves made sand. From sand I was ground into dust, and the arms of the wind carried me to the four corners of the world.

The rain brought me back to earth, and I felt humble. I became a beautiful flower, until time devoured me, petal, stem, root and color.

Finally, I was just a fragrance beneath a full moon, using her light to guide me to her kingdom.

Now I am delicate and ethereal. Silence is a joyful child flowing in my veins. No longer a reef lying in wait for ships, I am at peace.

THE PATH

N the landscape of a dream, I found myself before a mountain. At its summit was a light, shining like the sun reflected in a thousand mirrors. Drawn to it, I climbed until I found a cave from which that bright light and a fragrant aroma streamed.

I stepped inside and saw a splendid hall whose walls seemed to be painted with stardust. At its center was a flowering heart whose every beat emitted an exquisite perfume and a brilliant light.

Moving closer, I saw its outstretched arms. On the palms of its hands were written the following words:

Brother, every forced laugh leads to a scream.
There is no other way; this is the path.
This scream of fear is in every mouth.
Every mouth is a thirst and every thirst an emptiness.
Emptiness is loneliness; loneliness is silence.
Silence is nothing but a stifled scream.
This scream is an entreaty; an entreaty is a lament.
Every lament is fear, every fear a darkness.
Darkness is night; night has its stars.
A star is light; light shivers.
A shiver is coldness; the coldness is death.
Death is a tear, a tear that is divided.
The tear may become a forced smile again.
Or it may discover hope.
With hope it can climb towards its dreams.
Dreaming is magic; magic desire.
Desire is pleasure; pleasure is joy.
Joy is a smile, neither laughing nor crying.
There is no other way; this is the path.
How far you want to go depends on you
And how many times you want to walk the path.

THE GNOME'S PRAISE

*L*OST in the forest and surrounded by the shadows of night, Little Friend suddenly saw the light of a campfire. As he approached, to his surprise, he thought he saw a gnome, wrapped in solitude, who was talking to himself.

"There are tiny suns circling all around me, but they can't be seen. I am part of them; I am one of them; we are one. Meanwhile, time is turning, too. I am also time, and we are also one. It is mine, and I belong to it.

"All sounds lie like tiny murmuring drops of dew on the hills and valleys of my hearing. Everything I notice is like a graceful deer, walking with silken steps across the landscape of my penetrating vision.

"I am a moth circling my own flame. Sometimes my wings get burned and, as I fall, I am rescued by the upturned hands of my longing.

"But my thinking, my feeling, my loving could be even greater than they are. They haven't fully bloomed in me, just as they haven't bloomed in others.

"I am melancholy when I remember my beloved homeland – out there, where nothing meets everything, where the immense iridescent light of bliss makes one's gaze grow even wider. Out there where Mystery nourishes what is most profound. Out there where Light with no apparent source tunnels through the darkness and penetrates vast space where there is no single identifiable place. And still onward it travels – far beyond the universe, everlastingly, through eternity and infinity.

"Oh! Such a wealth of bliss in every particle of every thing. Oh, beloved earth, where there is no end. Where all is only a beginning. Where limitation is unknown. Where, one step beyond the horizon, all frontiers dissolve. Oh, beloved whirlwind, calmly carrying me at your center, you pass through every place, every time, every element. Oh, beloved point in the universe, I still remember you – a place of peace inside the great soul. Oh, union of nothing and everything, confronted by the wonder of the small and the great, your very essence is humility.

"I thank you for my little wings and small understanding – like a tiny drop of volcanic fire. I thank you for trusting me and revealing yourself to me. It has let me see and appreciate all the many manifestations of the spark of life. I am now born each dawn, and I continually live in you."

THE CANYON
OF SLEEPING ECHOES

LITTLE FRIEND traveled throughout the land in search of someone who might be able to tell him who he was and what he would become. But everyone he asked only talked about himself. Disappointed, he continued his search, hoping some day he would find satisfaction.

He recalled the Wind's words: "I am eternal, with the power to be gentle or to be as strong as a thousand wings. Once I unchain myself, I go freely wherever I wish."

The Flower had said: "I am fragile, and though I depend on water, earth, air, and light, I am free to give thanks with my perfume and beauty."

"I am like time," the Stream had said, "always the same, always different. Wherever I go, I am well received because I bring prosperity."

The last one he had questioned was the Sun, who had said: "I am the present, always constant, and wherever you find me, I am at once both fruit and seed."

Little Friend continued traveling through time, and one of the footprints he left behind muttered: "How much longer must I put up with this fellow who is like a canyon of sleeping echoes?"

THE RAINBOW

—— ◆ ——

wo lovers sitting face-to-face were talking to each other with their eyes. "I am complete because you give me the colors and light that give life to my dreams."

"The great joy of my soul is that you are the brush and the canvas with which I paint the picture of my life – and you are the reason I paint it."

And, as they talked to each other this way, the light they shared created a rainbow with a great treasure at either end.

THE WHATCHAMACALLIT REMOVERS

—— ◆ ——

NCE there were three Whatchamacallit removers. They worked day and night, without rest, trying to lighten the load that humanity carried on its shoulders.

One worked for the wealth and power he could get. Another for the applause and attention. And the third worked because every time he removed a Whatchamacallit a smile was born in his heart.

THE BIOGRAPHICAL SKETCH

*I*T all began in eternity, lost in space. Then I found myself here, looking around curiously and saying to the Wind: "The days fly by like horses galloping across time – some black, some white, some dappled. They trample the hours under foot, leaving them behind, forming a road disappearing into the distance."

"And you, Little Friend, are mounted on such steeds," replied the Wind. "Look closely at yourself. You are like a circus rider doing somersaults over and over again."

"I didn't come into the world to prance about on horses," I quickly objected, "even if they are beautiful and white with decorated manes."

"For your own good, Little Friend," the Wind advised, "don't complain like all the others or you will end up trampled beneath their hooves. Like the hours, you will be stretched out over the earth, making a road leading backward." The Wind vanished, leaving only a meditative whisper behind.

So I returned to where I belonged. Every day now, I sit in front of the mirror, powdering my face, donning my harlequin costume, doing my act – hoping to make others smile. But learning never ends. So many times I fall off my horse or I perform so badly that all I manage to do is cause tears.

THE KINGDOM OF THE ZOMBIES

*A*FTER some weeks, there was great unrest in the Kingdom of the Zombies. "How could this have happened to Rasma?" everyone was asking each other.

Meanwhile, Rasma danced through the streets, laughing jubilantly – until he fell flat on the ground. Then he tried to catch the wind, wanting to hold it in his hands, to talk to it, to call it Brother. When evening came, twilight rested on his face, and his lips were whispering a haunting melody.

As he walked along, with each step he would turn around to scrutinize the footprints that were following him. He spoke to them: "Hello, how are you? What's that you say? Of course! You're blazing a trail for others."

Some began to suspect that Rasma's behavior was a trick to avoid his duties as a citizen of the kingdom. Then one day, one of the Zombies came running out of the forest, screaming: "Rasma! Rasma's gone crazy!"

"What happened?" asked the others as they crowded around.

"There in the forest," the Zombie explained in a frightened voice, "Rasma passed right in front of me without seeing me. I followed him and, further on, he suddenly stopped and stood still for quite some time. He was looking upward. Then he began to take off his clothes, so I went up to him and asked if he was sick. 'Yes,' he replied, 'but not for much longer. This communion with nature will cure me, and I'll be a child again. Birds will perch on my shoulders, and I'll talk with the plants, the clouds, the stones, the trees, the caterpillar, the lightning, the rain, the log, the stream, the rainbow – and also with God.' Then he knelt on the grass and wept so that I could hardly hear him. 'Why do I have such a tiny bag for collecting such great and beautiful treasures?' I was very frightened, and I came running to tell you about it."

The Council of Elders convened to deal with this delicate issue. They came to the conclusion that Rasma, once such a good example in the Kingdom of the Zombies, now posed a serious threat to the community, especially to the young people. Rasma's punishment was the harshest they could give. He was banished from their world and condemned to live forever in the Land of the Living.

SAGETOWN

—— ◆ ——

ONCE upon a time Little Friend set out in search of wisdom because he had found – among other things – that white isn't always white and black isn't always black.

On one of the many roads he traveled, he met an old man who understood the heavy burden Little Friend was carrying and who told him of a town far away, surrounded by mountains, where everyone was wise.

Fascinated, Little Friend traveled without rest until, his eyes full of smiles, he found it. But standing guard was a sign that said:

> *Entry prohibited!*
> *Unless you come with open ears,*
> *Your heart in your hand,*
> *And truth upon your lips.*

Little Friend left immediately because, among the few things that he had learned for certain was that wisdom neither should nor could prohibit anything – especially when one doesn't know what someone may be searching for.

THE LOVERS

—— ◆ ——

THE Sun was waving a radiant goodbye when the Lover, his heart in his hand, said to his beloved: "Why, dearest love, when I offer you all that I am, do you spurn it, making it seem not enough?"

The maiden was silent for a moment. Then, gazing into infinity, she replied: "I have received many wounds on my path, and I have held them close to me like sisters so they wouldn't hurt so deeply. The worst of this is that I have lost my sensitivity, and I, too, have learned how to wound."

"Then I shall leave you," her sad Lover said, "carrying this thorn of yours inside me. However painful, it will shed light on my path, until I find someone who is able to remove it."

The maiden didn't hear what her Lover said. Instead, she heard: "Know this well. All things return to their proper resting place. Keep this in mind and try to mend what is broken within you."

The Lover was about to leave when his beloved stopped him. Now she could be his Lover, so she offered him her heart.

THE RACE

———— ✦ ————

A T the stroke of noon, a race took place between Little Friend and Mrs. Tortoise. Little Friend took it easy throughout the race, enjoying whatever caught his eye. Mrs. Tortoise, like the persistent drop of water that wears away a stone, just kept moving.

They went on like this until Little Friend crossed the finish line, winning by only a few steps.

"The winner is Mrs. Tortoise," the judge announced.

"But I finished first," Little Friend cried angrily.

"Perhaps you didn't read the rules of the contest," the judge replied. "Here they are for your information."

Little Friend read them and found that rule seven stated: "The winner shall be the one who, according to his or her capacity, makes the greater effort."

THE MANUSCRIPT OF LIFE

◆

If you wish to know about your	*You will find it in your*
Death	*Stagnation*
Evil	*Ignorance*
Hatred	*Losses*
Envy	*Dissatisfactions*
Fear	*Doubts*
Grief	*Weaknesses*
Tears	*Impotence*
Sadness	*Absences*
Loneliness	*Sterility*
Birth	*Knowledge*
Growth	*Meditation*
Satisfaction	*Achievements*
Wealth	*Inner Being*
Strength	*Ideals*
Power	*Decisions*
Life	*Visions*
Pleasure	*Happiness*
Peace	*Wisdom*
Love	*Freedom*
Freedom	*Creativity*

THE WORK OF WIND AND TIME

A MAN was walking along, bent with sorrow. The Wind approached him in a friendly way and asked: "Are you really suffering so much, my good man?"

Upset because his suffering was so obvious, the man replied: "Having dried my tears so many times before, why do you ask?"

"But that's exactly why I ask, Little Friend," the Wind replied. "True tears run so deep that I can't reach them. Drying them is the work of my brother, Time."

A NEW NAME FOR THE MENDER OF MASKS

LITTLE FRIEND went back once again to the Mender of Masks: "I have come to ask you to restore my mask – it's worn out."

Remembering that Little Friend had come to him countless times before, each time in a worse state than before, the Mender of Masks decided to give him a complete overhaul. He discovered the problem and fixed it.

From then on the Mender of Masks was known as the Mender of Hearts.

THE LETTER

THIS letter arrived on a gust of morning wind. Time had erased name and address. Maybe now this letter will find its way to the right person.

My Beloved Companion,

I sing praises to the many women who are one in you; to the valleys of your world, where I peacefully walk; to your rivers, on whose banks I quench my thirst; to the shores of your soul, where I find the flower of tenderness. I sing praises to your light, which makes me love you more each day; to your sweet hiding places, where I am your happy lover; to your infinite look of love and the warmth of your smile, which fill me with health and make me remember you everywhere I go.

I sing praises to the universes that are born in your womb; to your heart, which guards a thousand treasures; to your beating pulse, which fills me with peace and joy; to your voice, like dawn, where harmonies are born; to the universe you have created for the communion of our souls.

I sing praises to your body, which is my own blood; to your lips, from which I drink dreams; to the undying continuous present that forms our love; to your fields of wheat, which grow and become the bread that nourishes me; and to this understanding of freedom, that wherever I walk I am in the realm of your desire.

I sing praises to your tears of love and sadness, shed for this dear humanity, whose wings are sometimes fearful of the wind.

I sing praises to your song, which shatters silence; to your language of sun, which illuminates my senses; to your unequaled majesty, to which I offer my dreams and hopes.

I dedicate this song of love to you, my dearly beloved, because you have performed this miracle that lets me grow and flower, through which I live and through which I can truly be myself.

Thank you.

Your Loving Companion

THE OPENER OF DOORS

HE village idiot was called the Opener of Doors because every day he told the following story:

"The first door I opened was the door of Crying. The next one was the door of Light, which hurt my eyes. Then I opened other doors, one for each of my senses. The door of Day followed and then Night. Then the door of my own body's movement. Opening the strange doors of Thinking and Imagination, I flew through worlds whose inhabitants went about smiling at each other, sustaining each other with peaceful looks. Their many hands were sowing seeds for a future harvest of desire.

"When I opened the unchanging door of Time, I found myself face-to-face with the need to develop my reasoning powers. It was hard to cross that threshold because of all the false things I had been told and because of the inertia I felt when I realized I would have to figure things out for myself. And so I reached the door of Mist and Fog, the door of the Abyss, and then the door of Silence whose sound pierced me to the core.

"It was when I opened the door of the Profound that I discovered how to see with new eyes. Behind every door lay four more, one facing each of the four directions. I was in the center and had the choice of opening any one of them. There was a fifth door. I couldn't see it, but I could feel it somewhere near.

"One day – one of those days in which marvelous things happen – a great joy flooded through me. The fifth door appeared at last. I opened it and went through. All I can say is that I have never known a better place. Its peace transformed me into something new and timeless. I saw beyond color, becoming color itself. I felt I was living in eternal music that came from everywhere.

"Then I awoke. It was all a dream and yet, because of this dream, I now know the fifth door exists. I can choose this best of doors, and I can always find it."

The Opener of Doors was heard to repeat this story every day. Time passed, and one day the village idiot was no longer to be found. After that, those who had never opened the doors of their hearing and understanding felt they were missing some keys from their key rings.

BLINDNESS

—— ◆ ——

*L*ITTLE FRIEND was desperately trying to flee a hostile forest, and crying seemed to be his only escape. "I need a light, just a little one, to illuminate my steps!"

"If you were the Sun," he heard a voice say, "it's conceivable that you could make a light as bright as day. But since you continue to create Night, you can give birth only to darkness."

The voice was that of Little Friend's Shadow, who was dressed in rags. "I wish that we could change places sometime," it continued, "so you could know how ruinous it is to lack freedom – what it's like to be at the mercy of blind men like you."

DESERT WASTES

—— ◆ ——

*W*HILE traveling through the forest of life, Little Friend, tired and thirsty, threw himself face down at the edge of a deep pool. He saw an unshaven, haggard, lifeless face with bulging eyes reflected in the crystal mirror of the water. He struck out at it, crying: "I am tired of being a loser, tired of idle talk, tired of being constantly tripped up by the rocks and brambles of life."

When the water regained its calm surface, the Image reappeared and said: "Don't complain about losing things or stumbling or taking a fall. This is the price you pay for experience, and experience is worth more than you know."

Hardly listening, Little Friend went on looking at his reflection in the water. He sadly pondered the lifeless look of his hands, feet, eyes, ears, mouth and his heart. "I am so many deserts wrapped up in one," he thought.

And in unison, his Deserts chanted: "That means we are vast and rich."

"Vast and rich?" Little Friend smiled ironically.

"The desert is the only thing that has room to contain everything," his Deserts answered. "It is like someone who knows himself to be ignorant and seeks to fill himself with knowledge so he can become fertile."

THE RUNNER

◆

NCE there was a runner, and every day he could be seen running from north to south and from east to west. When asked why he was always running, he replied that he was trying to catch Love.

Each time he thought he was about to capture his elusive prey, he produced a burst of speed that brought him close. But it was never enough to make the catch.

One day, exhausted, the runner heard the voice of Love speaking to him from within: "The way to catch me is to help your fellow beings." So the runner set about to serve his neighbors, but Love, as elusive as ever, remained beyond his grasp.

Despairing of ever attaining his goal, the runner found himself overlooking a valley, and he sat down. Looking below, he remembered seeing a little boy playing happily, a contented mother with enough bread for her children and an old woman, a stranger to the song of life, saying her rosary. Each bead brought a smile to her face.

As he watched these scenes from his memory, the runner's eyes softened. His face became a smile, and a great feeling of happiness welled up within him. A hand that was not his appeared and pointed toward the valley. "These scenes you have painted are quite beautiful, aren't they? That's why I have accompanied you on your journey."

"Why haven't I seen you before?" the runner asked, with an even bigger smile.

"You weren't able to see me because you were helping others in the hope of being rewarded. But now you know that the hope of reward is not what loving is."

TELL

— ◆ —

THE last time Little Friend saw the person he had known as the Painter's Apprentice was early one morning when the sun and moon were face-to-face. By then, the Painter's Apprentice was thought to be out of his mind. Seeing Little Friend, he approached him, looking lost. He laid his right hand on Little Friend's shoulder and, with a sweet, melodious voice that came from the depths of his being, said:

"Brother, tell your Heart to allow dreams without number to be born and to let me tell it of distant stars, unknown worlds and newly created universes.

"Tell your Hands to let me tell them about comets the size of a thumb, about solar systems grander than our own, within our very veins.

"Tell your Eyes to let me tell them about nebulae full of radiant spheres, about infinities of heavenly bodies on the other side of our dreams.

"Tell your Mind to let me tell it the story of all stories about eternity, beyond space and time, in which lies that which is, that which has been, that which remains to be, that which those who have walked through the door of matter have discovered.

"Tell your Ear to let me tell it that, to travel this way, you must become good friends with the meteors who are free in the queenly galaxy. This galaxy is a sphere and, entering it, you can find the point where the extremes of beginning and end are joined. At the heart of this sphere all energies are harmoniously one.

"Tell your Path to let me tell it the truth, that all is dust, millions of particles, flowing in and out. Some are small because they can't surrender to their highest task. Some are large because their actions are based in peace, the fruit of universal wisdom. From this polished sphere, a living unity, the essence of all existence is distilled.

"Tell your cosmic spark of Love to let me tell it about these and many more things, born every day from our mother, Light, who illuminates our spiritual core.

"But, if they don't want me to tell them all this, then at least let my thirst be satisfied by drinking from the Light that is there in your universe."

ABOUT THE PATH

A T a certain meeting, I got to know a bearded man, who made quite an impression with his ivory-colored tunic and a scepter in his right hand. Some of those present asked him to speak about the path. This is what he said:

"There is a way of looking that is not looking. We make ourselves small and travel over the shining crystals of the mind. From there, we can see the road stretching from one end of the horizon to the other. And there, on that very thin line, is the path of both body and spirit. This trinity of Path-Body-Spirit causes us to be, at every moment, at the center of four different roads, one leading forward, one backward, one upward and one downward.

"To go forward is to be in the continuous present and to see, to be able to analyze both the past and the future. This road is useful for understanding others, as well as ourselves, and it helps us prevent other times from clashing with the time in which we really live. We learn that every clash, conflict or disharmony is caused by the meeting of two different forces, times, temperatures or concepts.

"But it often happens that a clash between two opposites does not always have a negative effect. The meeting of warm and cold currents in the sea gives rise to plankton, which is food for the fish. The joining of anode and cathode produces light. The union of man and woman gives birth to a new and perfect body.

"To go backward is not necessarily to retreat. This road can be like a sieve through which we filter impurities and prepare ourselves for overcoming any obstacles that may arise.

"To climb upward to our own summit is to meditate and ask why, so that we find our own answers. It is to search for ourselves in the majesty of worlds both small and large, until we reach what is perpetual and universal.

"To go downward is to cover oneself in shadows and to enter the abyss of death. In most cases, we do this without wanting to. But, even if we're inexperienced, our intelligence makes it a fruitful journey. And we emerge strengthened, with our shining torches held high. When we have buried our dark selves, we can then walk the path of a richer, more valuable life."

BEING FULLY ALIVE

HE night was covered with a vast mantle of moonlight. It was a time when the young were gathered around the campfire to listen to the wise old man who was helping their souls to mature.

"How shall we recognize the moment when we are most alive?" Little Friend asked him.

"You will know," the wise old man replied, "when a tear of happiness runs down your cheek. It will be your expression of gratitude."

"But I thought tears were a sign of grief."

"Just because you only half understand something now, Little Friend, doesn't mean that what remains won't someday be revealed."

CONCERNING THE STAR POLISHER'S PROFESSION

◆

ONCE while traveling, I came across three star polishers. I asked each one of them in turn why he had chosen that profession.

The first replied he had done so because it gave him the opportunity to see his own reflection every day. The second said he had chosen it because his ancestors had always polished stars.

The third said: "I am a polisher of stars because I've noticed that often they are guiding lights for someone who has lost his way. But I really do it because I want to become a master star polisher. Then I will be prepared for the day when I meet my own star."